SMALL *Oxford* BOOKS

WINE

SMALL *Oxford* BOOKS

WINE

Compiled by
JOHN ARLOTT

Oxford New York
OXFORD UNIVERSITY PRESS
1984

Oxford University Press, Walton Street, Oxford OX2 6DP

*London Glasgow New York Toronto
Delhi Bombay Calcutta Madras Karachi
Kuala Lumpur Singapore Hong Kong Tokyo
Nairobi Dar es Salaam Cape Town
Melbourne Auckland*

*and associated companies in
Beirut Berlin Ibadan Mexico City Nicosia*

Oxford is a trade mark of Oxford University Press

British Library Cataloguing in Publication Data

Arlott, John
Wine.—(Small Oxford books)
1. Wine and wine making.
I. Title
641.2′2   TP548
ISBN 0-19-214146-5

Library of Congress Cataloging in Publication Data

Arlott, John.
Wine.—(Small Oxford books)
Includes index.
1. Wine and wine making.   I. Title.
TP548.A73 1984   641.2′22   83–13294
ISBN 0-19-214146-5

❀

In grateful memory of

Richard Aldington
Daniel Querre
Raymond Postgate

who led me to wine

*Set by New Western Printing Ltd.
Printed in Great Britain by
Hazell Watson & Viney Limited
Aylesbury, Bucks*

Introduction

Wine is man's most successful effort to translate the perishable into the permanent. Cheese, of course, is a more widely spread attempt; but it can never come so near to permanence as, for instance, the Rudesheimer Apostelwein of 1727 which was still flavoursome when it was drunk in 1973.

Although wine originated in the Near East and is deeply enshrined in the Bible and English literature, it is almost entirely the province of Western – especially Mediterranean – man. Its second main area of production and consumption is South America; while the twentieth century has seen immense progress in its making and drinking in North America, Russia, Australia and even Japan. On the other hand, the bulk of the world's population, in Asia, and in Africa between the vineyards of the Mediterranean coastal strip and those of the Cape, and, by religious law, the Muslim nations, have little appetite for it.

It is most truly part of domestic life in the Mediterranean countries, to such an extent that convicts in Italian prisons are entitled to a daily ration of wine by human right. Indeed, the Italian, French, Spanish, Portuguese or Greek peasant takes wine – out of an unlabelled and undesignated bottle – with his meals as a matter of course. It is not, to him, the product of a named vineyard; but simply wine; as a Dane, a Belgian or Englishman regards beer.

The increasing publication over the last two decades of books on the subject in English indicates the growing interest – perhaps more self-conscious and literary than in the true wine countries, but nevertheless unmistakable – in traditionally beer and spirit drinking countries.

Attitudes to wine have long varied widely; from religious and state-dictated prohibition and strongly preached abstinence, to a degree of tolerance which has latterly moved some to alarm at the social and economic consequences of alcoholism. Wine emerges fairly well from that disquiet. In Russia, where the consumption of spirits has produced such dire effects that the government seriously considered enforcing prohibition, such immense steps have been taken to wean the population from vodka to wine as may make the USSR both the world's biggest producer, and biggest importer of wine by the middle 1990s. There is, indeed, a widening recognition of the fact, long appreciated by reasonable people, that moderate wine drinking is an acceptable aspect of civilized living.

There is a considerable gap of appreciation between the Italian labourer, to whom the glass in his hand is simply 'vino', and the connoisseur – often of a country where wine is not an accepted domestic product – who sniffs at his glass of Château Cheval Blanc 1947 with a background of palate memory, knowledge, and comparative standards. Who shall say which is the truer appreciation?

It is, though, beyond argument that wine offers many more pleasures than simply that of drinking. As the tasting expert instructs, the eye and the nose should appreciate it before the palate. It lends itself, though, to discussion, reminiscence and, as these extracts demonstrate, to humour, wisdom, and the heightening of delight.

Six bibliographies in English alone testify to the extent of the literature of wine. The books extend over viticulture, oenology, chemistry, law, history, particular wine regions, vineyards, and appreciation. In this century emphasis has shifted from the agricultural, through a semi-romantic period, to a harder, historical, technical and critical vein.

Always, too, there has been a strain of contemplation, echoing an almost lyric quality of enjoyment; of which

Lord Byron was the laureate, but by no means the only poet.

The lore of wine is full of character; for the essential reason – *in vino veritas* – that wine brings out the true characteristics of the drinker; and drunkenness exaggerates them to the point of caricature.

Drinkers, of course, are not simply as different as human beings; but their differences are heightened by drink; and the more relishable for that. Writing about drink runs the gamut from rude humour, and warm humanity, through wit, history, description, technology, perception, appreciation, to high poetry.

Wine is as good as life to a man, if it be drunk moderately: what is life then to a man that is without wine? For it was made to make men glad.

Ecclesiasticus 31: 27

Invitation to Drink

Wine drinking in modern Britain owes more to André Simon than to any other one man. He came from France in his twenties to settle in England. He entered the wine trade before the First World War – in which he fought with the French army – and, after it, not only founded the Wine and Food Society but, through his writings and lectures, created a whole fresh British attitude towards gastronomy in general, and wine in particular. Impressively lucid writer in what was for him a second language, he communicated capably on the elementary, as well as the sophisticated, level of drinking. In this passage he is, characteristically, both missionary and expository.

Water, like air, is indispensable; wine is not, but it is desirable. Wherever men have chosen to settle and live, they have first of all made quite sure that there was a supply of water, but whenever they have attained a higher measure of civilisation or culture, they have always spent a good deal of their time, labour and hard-earned money that they and theirs might drink wine. It is true that wine is a food, and that its food value is greater, as well as richer in vitamins, than other fruit juices, but there are many other foods available which cost appreciably less than wine. The chief appeal which wine has always had and still has for all intelligent people is due to its specific action upon the nervous system; wine is both soothing and stimulating; it is a joy and a solace; it may become a habit, but never a craving.

There are wines beyond count, because there are an immense number of different species of vines grown in a very considerable number of vineyards all the world over, under varying climatic conditions from year to year. If you multiply the number of different sorts of grapes from which wine is made by the number of different people who press those grapes, attend to the fermentation of their sweet juice, and care for it until it be ready to drink, you will easily realise that there must be such a number of different wines to choose from that it should be possible to enjoy the right wine for the right occasion and at the right price, did you but know where to look for it.

There are wines which are excellent before, after or between meals, but by far the great majority of all wines are best with food; they taste better with food and food never tastes so good as with the right wine. Wine and food are natural partners, ideal partners when well matched.

Wine deserves and repays to be approached with enthusiasm and intelligence, and to be handled and served with care, not the hireling's care, but the connoisseur's loving care.

Of course, there are many people who lead blameless lives and who drink no wine, listen to no music, read no poetry, look at no pictures; they happen to have been born without any artistic sense whatever, just like the more unfortunate among us who happen to be born blind or deaf. Happily, however, the great majority of rich and poor alike possess normal senses of sight, hearing, smell and taste, all of them given to us to be trained as we grow up and grow old that we may the better enjoy our days. Do not imagine that the appreciation of wine is a reserved occupation for experts only. It is not so. The common man has every chance of becoming a wine connoisseur, although it is quite obvious that if he be a poor man he must inevitably be greatly handicapped by the present prices of wine. But the poor man with a palate is much better off than the rich man who has not got one, since he may possibly be rich one day, and still have a palate, whilst the rich man who may be poor one day will never have any taste.

To become a wine-connoisseur one must drink good wine, not necessarily great wines, but sound and honest wine, with sufficient concentration to memorise its colour, *bouquet* or fragrance, and flavour: in other words one must cultivate a 'palate memory'. Just as it is always a pleasure to recognise the features or the voice of a friend, there is a very real satisfaction in recognising a wine which one has tasted and enjoyed before.

Whatever its price may be, wine surely is worth more than the money that it costs to buy when it brings joy to your home, the joy of sunshine.

André Simon, *How to Enjoy Wine*, 1952

In yet another preface he is equally wise and persuasive.

Wine is best because it is the safest, pleasantest and most wholesome of all beverages. It is safer than water or milk: you cannot get typhoid or T.B. from any wine, be it old or young, cheap and nasty, or rare and costly. No microbes live in wine. It is pleasanter than other safe drinks because it is more gentle as well as more varied. There is no wine without any alcohol, since grape juice does not begin to be wine until it has fermented, and by then the sugar of the grape juice has become the alcohol of the wine. But the alcohol in wine is as the canvas upon which an artist paints a picture: it is there, of course, but you do not see it and do not think of it; it is not the canvas that you are interested in, but the picture which is on it. It is the same with wine; it is not the small percentage of alcohol that appeals to you, but the brilliant ruby of the wine's colour, the attractive perfume of its 'bouquet' and the delicious savour of its 'farewell,' the lingering taste which it leaves behind as it descends smoothly down your grateful throat: that is the picture that is painted on the canvas of the wine's alcohol. Of course the alcohol is there all the time, and very welcome it is: it holds everything so well together; it diffuses such a comforting light and warmth; it provides the limelight which enables us to enjoy fully all the fine points of the wine's colour, bouquet and flavour. And it does it in a gentle fashion; it is never brutal; it never is treacherous, stabbing one in the back or in the brain as immature spirits do. Wine is 'a good familiar creature,' as Shakespeare calls it, and Shakespeare always is right. Wine is a gentle stimulant, a good counsellor, a true friend, who neither bores nor irritates us: it does not send us to sleep, nor does it keep us awake; it never becomes a craving or a tyrant; it is always ready to cheer, to help, but not to bully us.

André Simon, A *Wine Primer*, 1946

Many, of course, are introduced to the concept of wine by the account of the Miracle at Cana.

And the third day there was a marriage in Cana of Galilee; and the mother of Jesus was there:

And both Jesus was called, and his disciples, to the marriage.

And when they wanted wine, the mother of Jesus saith unto him, 'They have no wine.'

Jesus saith unto her, 'Woman, what have I to do with thee? Mine hour is not yet come.'

His mother saith unto the servants, 'Whatsoever he saith unto you, do it.'

And there were set there six waterpots of stone, after the manner of the purifying of the Jews, containing two or three firkins apiece.

Jesus saith unto them, 'Fill the waterpots with water.' And they filled them up to the brim.

And he saith unto them, 'Draw out now, and bear unto the governor of the feast.' And they bare it.

When the ruler of the feast had tasted the water that was made wine and knew not whence it was: (but the servants which drew the water knew;) the governor of the feast called the bridegroom.

And saith unto him, 'Every man at the beginning doth set forth good wine; and when men have well drunk, then that which is worse: but though hast kept the good wine until now.'

This beginning of miracles did Jesus in Cana of Galilee, and manifested forth his glory; and his disciples believed on him.

St John 2: 1–11

(An event crystallized by the poet J. D. Beazley into 'The conscious water saw its God and blushed'.)

The pleasures of wine are a theme through much of literature, especially classic poetry: Greek –

> To-day I'll haste to quaff my wine
> As if to-morrow ne'er should shine;
> And if to-morrow comes, why then—
> I'll haste to quaff my wine again.
> And thus while all our days are bright,
> Nor time has dimmed their bloomy light,
> Let us the festal hours beguile
> With mantling cup and cordial smile;
> And shed from every bowl of wine
> The richest drop on Bacchus' shrine.

For Death may come, with brow unpleasant,
May come when least we wish him present,
And beckon to the sable shore
And grimly, bid us—taste no more.

Anaecreon, Odes, c. 545 BC

The same thought was echoed in Rome:

'Why linger outside, wearied with the heat of summer,
when you might sink on soft green couches of grass?
Here are flower-laden nooks and leafy arbours, mixing
cups, lyres, lutes, and cool alcoves, shaded by foliage
...Here, too, is wine cool from the earthenware jar,
and a stream whose babbling water runs trippingly
with husky murmur...Boy, bring wine and dice. Let
tomorrow seek its own salvation! Death, twitching
the ear, cries: "Enjoy your life: I come!"'

Virgil, The Copa, 23 BC

*Well known, but too fine to be described as hackneyed,
is this great wine stanza:*

O, for a draught of vintage! that hath been
  Cool'd a long age in the deep-delved earth,
Tasting of Flora and the country-green,
  Dance, and Provençal song, and sunburnt mirth!
O for a beaker full of the warm South,
  Full of the true, the blushful Hippocrene,
    With beaded bubbles winking at the brim,
      And purple-stained mouth;
That I might drink, and leave the world unseen,
  And with thee fade away into the forest dim.

John Keats, 'Ode to a Nightingale', 1820

[6]

The Persian in similar vein is later, but it echoes earlier thought; and it comes from the land where the first evidence of wine-making was discovered:

Ah, my Beloved, fill the Cup that clears
Today of past Regrets and Future Fears:
   To-morrow. Why, To-morrow I may be
Myself with Yesterday's Sev'n thousand Years.

For some we loved, the loveliest and the best
That from his Vintage rolling Time hath prest,
   Have drunk their Cup a Round or two before,
And one by one crept silently to rest.

. . .

Then to his earthen bowl did I adjourn
My lip to the secret well of life to learn:
   And Lip to Lip it murmured – 'While you live
Drink! For once dead you never shall return.'

> *The Rubáiyát of Omar Khayyám, c.* 1100,
> trans. Edward Fitzgerald, 1859

Wine was celebrated, too, in China:

If Heaven did not love wine,
There would be no wine star in Heaven.
If Earth did not love wine
There would be no wine springs on earth –
Why then be ashamed before Heaven to love wine?
I have heard that clear wine is like the Sages;
But then it is said that thick wine is like the
   Virtuous Worthies.
Why should we strive to be gods and immortals?
Three cups, and one can perfectly understand the
   Great Tao;
A gallon and one is in accord with all nature.
Only those in the midst of it can completely
   comprehend the joys of wine:
I do not proclaim them to be sober.

> Li T'ai Po, *c.* AD 740

The Apocrypha holds many worthwhile thoughts on the subject:

Give strong drink unto him that is ready to perish, and wine unto those that be of heavy hearts.

Let him drink and forget his poverty and remember his misery no more.

Ecclesiasticus 31: 6, 7

It was Anacreon, again, who produced one of the livelier arguments in favour of (wine) drinking; and, in this case, was fortunate in his English translator.

The thirsty earth soaks up the rain,
And drinks, and gapes for drink again.
The plants suck in the earth, and are
With constant drinking fresh and fair;
The sea itself – which one would think
Should have but little need of drink –
Drinks ten thousand rivers up,
So filled that they o'erflow the cup.
The busy sun – and one would guess
By 's drunken fiery face no less –
Drinks up the sea, and when he's done,
The moon and stars drink up the sun:
They drink and dance by their own light,
They drink and revel all the night.
Nothing in nature's sober found,
But an eternal health goes round.
Fill up the bowl then, fill it high,
Fill up the glasses there; for why
Should every creature drink but I;
Why, man of morals, tell me why?

Translated by Abraham Cowley, *c.* 1656

There is similar, but gentler, warmth in these lines of roughly the same period:

Tonight grave sir, both my poor house and I
Do equally desire your company ...

Digestive cheese and fruit there sure will be
But that which most doth my Muse and me
Is a rare cup of rich canary wine
Which is the Mermaid's now, but shall be mine
Of which had Horace or Anaecreon tasted
Their lives, as do their lines, till now had lasted.
Tobacco, Nectar, or the Thespian spring
Are all but Luther's beer to this I sing.
Of this we will sup free, but moderately,
And we will have no Polly or Parrot by;
Nor shall our cups make any guilty men:
But at our parting we shall be as when
We innocently met. No simple word
That shall be uttered at our mirthful board
Shall make us sad next morning, or affright
The liberty that we'll enjoy to-night.

Ben Jonson, 'Inviting a Friend to Supper', 1616

*These lines, too, were originally written in Latin, but
by an Englishman (and a don at Oxford) with an
appetite also for tobacco – he wrote on that subject, too.*

If all be true that I do think,
There are five reasons we should drink;
Good wine – a friend – or being dry –
Or lest we should be, by and by –
Or any other reason why!

Henry Aldrich, 'Five Reasons for Drinking', 1705

[9]

There is, perhaps, a rounder satisfaction in this much later piece:

> If I drink water whilst this doth last,
> May I never again drink wine:
> For how can a man, in his life of a span,
> Do anything better than dine?
> We'll dine and drink, and say if we think
> That anything better can be;
> And when we have dined, wish all mankind
> May dine as well as we.

Thomas Love Peacock

The same connoisseur produced this argument:

There are two reasons for drinking: one is, when you are thirsty, to cure it: the other, when you are not thirsty, to prevent it ... prevention is better than cure.

Thomas Love Peacock, Melincourt, 1817

Still, though, the relaxed wine drinker (doing his best to forget the destruction of the wine bottles in Teheran in 1979) returns to what must seem to him the ultimate wisdom on the subject, to the old Persian.

Come, fill the Cup, and in the Fire of Spring
The Winter Garment of Repentance fling:
    The Bird of Time has but a little way
To fly – and Lo ! the Bird is on the Wing.

. . .

And lately by the tavern door agape,
Came stealing through the dusk an angel shape
    Bearing a vessel on his shoulder; and
He bid me taste of it; and 'twas – the grape!

The grape that can with logic absolute
The two and seventy jarring sects confute:
    The subtle alchemist that in a trice
Life's leaden metal into gold transmute.

. . .

How long, how long, in infinite pursuit
Of This and That endeavour and dispute?
　Better be merry with the fruitful Grape
Than sadden after none, or bitter, Fruit.

> *The Rubáiyát of Omar Khayyám, c.* 1100,
> trans. Edward Fitzgerald, 1859

*The classic poets are not always translated in their own
spirit but often rather slavishly into verse. Is wine
inspiration?*

> If with water you fill up your glasses,
> You'll never write anything wise
> But wine is the horse of Parnassus,
> That carries a bard to the skies.

> Athenaeus, *Deipnosophistai, c.* AD 200

*One bard – poet in prose – could look at it more
earthily:*

I drink eternally. This is to me an eternity of drinking
and drinking of eternity ... I moisten my windpipe
with wine – I drink to banish all fear of dying –
Drink but deep enough and you shall live for ever. If
the parchment on which is endorsed my bonds and
bills could drink as well as I, my creditors would never
need to buy wine when I settle my just dues.

> François Rabelais, *Gargantua and Pantagruel,*
> 1534–64

*There have been those, too, who believed that drinking
was the way to glory:*

He that eateth well, drinketh well; he that drinketh
well, sleepeth well; sinneth not; he that sinneth not
goeth straight through Purgatory to Paradise.

> William Lithgow, *Poems,* 1640

*Quite forty years earlier, though, one of several varia-
tions on a theme by John Minsheu (fl. 1599) indicated
the same route:*

Good wine makes good blood,
Good blood causeth good humours,
Good humours cause good thoughts,
Good thoughts bring forth good works,
Good works carry a man to heaven.
   Ergo,
Good wine carrieth a man to heaven.

Some critics see more merit in wine than other drinks.

Lo! the poor toper whose untutor'd sense,
Sees bliss in ale, and can with wine dispense;
Whose head proud fancy never taught to steer,
Beyond the muddy ecstasies of beer.

     George Crabbe, 'Imitation of Pope', 1820(?)

There is a warmth about much of the praise of wine –

Wine that maketh glad the heart of man.
         Psalm 104, 15

The same idea lay in the mind of Homer.

And wine can of their wits the wise beguile,
Make the sage frolic and the serious smile.
      Odyssey, Book 4, c. 9th century BC

Once, too, a true poet tossed a truly poetic aside into a letter –

Give me books, fruit, French wine, fine weather and a little music out of doors, played by somebody I do not know.

   John Keats, Letter to Fanny Keats, 29 August 1819

Drink to-day, and drown all sorrow,
You shall perhaps not do it to-morrow;
Best, while you have it, use your breath;
There is no drinking after death.

Wine works the heart up, wakes the wit,
There is no cure 'gainst age but it;

It helps the headache, cough, and tisic,
And is for all diseases physic.

Then let us swill, boys, for our health;
Who drinks well, loves the commonwealth.
And he that will to bed go sober
Falls with the leaf still in October.

John Fletcher, 'The Bloody Brother', 1615(?)

It belongs in imagery on many levels:

A man not old, but mellow, like good wine.

Stephen Phillips, *Ulysses*, 1902

Webster went a little further:

Is not old wine wholesomest, old pippins
toothsomest,
Old wood burn brightest, old linen wash whitest?
Old soldiers, sweethearts, are surest, and old
lovers are soundest.

John Webster, *Westward Hoe*, 1607

*Sometimes it may be thought that the poets overplay
their hands. They can, though, on this theme, seek the
aid of one of the most learned of all literary scholars
and a considerable writer upon the subject of wine.*

There is absolutely no scientific proof, of a trustworthy
kind, that moderate consumption of sound alcoholic
liquor does a healthy body any harm at all; while on
the other hand there is the unbroken testimony of all
history that alcoholic liquors have been used by the
strongest, wisest, handsomest, and in every way best
races of all times, and the personal experience of in-
numerable individuals in favour of the use. One of the
most amazing audacities of these fanatics is the assertion that 'even moderate drinking shortens life'. A
moment's thought will show any clear-headed person
that this cannot be proved without an exhaustive bio-
logical and clinical record of every moderate drinker

since the beginning of time, unless there is a sophistic
'sometimes' slipped in, which renders the proposition
practically valueless.[1] Stopping a horse in order to
save someone else's life sometimes shortens the stopper's; and going to church on an inclement morning
may do so. Moreover, that moderate drinking *always*
shortens life, while it is insusceptible of proof, is, and
must ever be, susceptible of *dis*proof. Everyone knows,
or may know if he chooses, instances of moderate
drinkers who have reached ages far beyond the average
age of man, in a condition of bodily health which
compares with that of most, and of intellectual fitness
which should shame that of nearly all, teetotallers.
One supposes that this monstrous inexactitude is
founded on some kind of physiological experiment: and
indeed, if you give, say, a mouse, even a small quantity
of absinthe, or raw potato spirit, you probably may
say that, 'moderate' drinking has shortened life. But
otherwise the statement is one which no honest man
should make, except as one of opinion, and no rational
man credit, either as opinion or fact.

George Saintsbury, *Notes on a Cellar Book*, 1920

1 'Quantification of the predicate' has been scoffed at.
But in political logic it would often be valuable, and in
the above instance it is a touchstone.

The range of the poet's justification – and even his logic
– is wide:

> And much as Wine has played the Infidel,
> And robbed me of my Robe of Honour – well,
> I often wonder what the Vinters buy
> One half so precious as the goods they sell.

> *The Rubáiyát of Omar Khayyám, c.* 1100
> trans. Edward Fitzgerald, 1859

The drinker always returns to the poets, not merely for
poetry, but for confirmation, such as the charming
invitation in verse from a Laureate.

> You'll have no scandal while you dine,
> But honest talk and wholesome wine.

> Alfred Lord Tennyson, Letter to the Revd. F. D.
> Maurice, 1853

When argument is needed, it is not far to seek; a
scholar, novelist, biographer, classical translator and
perceptive drinker laid down these simple lines on its
merits and pleasures:

Wine is drunk for immediate pleasure first, and to
attain after that a general feeling of well-being, in
which the mind is placid but lively, the emotions are
friendly, and the body calm and satisfied. In wine
drinking, consequently, three faculties are involved:
Sight, Smell, Taste...

This is the way to drink wine.

Pour the wine, steadily and not splashily, into the
glass, filling it only two-thirds full. Then use the
faculty of sight; look at it. This is why the glass should
be colourless. You have paid for, and should enjoy, the
fine yellow of a big hock or of a sauternes, the pale
straw-like yellow of a manzanilla sherry, the dark heavy
red of a burgundy, or that curious fading colour of an
ageing claret. At the edge of the glass in this case the
red of the wine fades almost to grey, to colourlessness.
Observe, too, if the wine is muddy, and not, as it
should be, brilliantly clear.

Next, use the sense of *smell*. Hold the glass in your hand and rotate the wine gently. (This is why it must only be filled two-thirds full.) Then hang your nose over the edge of it and sniff. This is why the glass must come together at the rim, to collect the smell and present it respectfully to your nostrils. It is difficult not to be lyrical over the bouquet of a good wine. Tokay smells like green grass and weeds, trampled underfoot in a lush meadow. A full burgundy has a scent so strong it may make you dizzy; in its compound of flavours you can imagine violets and blackberries. A hock or moselle smells like a large bouquet of midsummer flowers. A claret is usually more delicate: its scents seem (but this may be fanciful) to succeed one another, like a chorus mincing across the stage. Moreover, the bouquet, too, may be a warning as well as a pleasure. A nasty wine, such as a bad sherry, tells your nose before you taste it. It stinks and you know there is villainy. Pour it into the potted plant and ask your host, next round, for gin.

Thirdly, use the sense of *taste*. Raise the glass to your mouth, take a small mouthful and roll it round your mouth. Let it irrigate the teeth and give the taste-buds of your tongue and palate time to notice and consider the first and second tastes that a wine usually has. Hold it in the mouth long enough to breathe in and out once through the nose. Then swallow, and you will often find that there is a third and last taste that it gives you as a farewell as it passes your tonsils. Then, after a moment of consideration, take a second larger mouthful if the wine deserves it. That is why the glass must be reasonably large; thimbles are a nuisance.

All this may sound a lot of trouble; and it is true that not all wines deserve it. But even with indifferent wines the careful drinker will stop for a moment to classify them, so to speak, before he puts them down. For the rest, all this procedure is merely a way of increasing your pleasure. It requires attention, but so do all pleasures. In fact, attentiveness is part of the nature of pleasure; an unobserved pleasure is not a pleasure at all.

Raymond Postgate, *The Plain Man's Guide to Wine*, 1951

A similar case, going a little further through the still, is argued by the greatest of the gastronomes:

A thing of enormous interest is that sort of instinct, as general as it is imperious, which leads us in search of strong drinks.

Wine, the most delightful of drinks, whether we owe it to Noah, who planted the vine, or to Bacchus, who pressed juice from the grape, dates from the childhood of the world; and beer, which is attributed to Osiris, goes back to a period beyond which nothing certain is known.

All men, even those it is customary to call savages, have been so tormented by this craving for strong drinks, that they have always managed to obtain them, however limited the extent of their knowledge.

They have turned the milk of their domestic animals sour, or extracted juice from various fruits and roots which they suspected of containing the elements of fermentation; and wherever human society has existed, we find that men were provided with strong liquors, which they used at their feasts, sacrifices, marriages, or funerals, in short on all occasions of merry-making or solemnity.

Wine was drunk and its praises sung for many centuries before men guessed at the possibility of extracting the spirituous part which makes its strength; but when the Arabs taught us the art of distillation, which they had invented for the purpose of extracting the scent of flowers, and above all that of the rose which occupies such an important place in their writings, then men began to believe that it was possible to discover in wine the cause of that special savour which has such a stimulating influence on the organ

of taste; and so, step by step, alcohol, spirits of wine, and brandy were discovered.

Alcohol is the prince of liquids, and carries the palate to its highest pitch of exaltation; its various preparations have opened up a new source of pleasure; it invests certain medicaments with a power which they could not otherwise have attained; and it has even become a formidable weapon in our hands, for the nations of the New World have been subdued and destroyed almost as much by brandy as by firearms.

The method by which alcohol was discovered has led to other important results; for consisting as it does in the separation and exposure of the parts which make up a body, and distinguish that body from all others, it has served as a model to scholars pursuing analogous researches; and they have made known to us entirely new substances, such as strychnine, quinine, morphine, and others, both discovered and to be discovered in the future.

Be that as it may, this thirst for a kind of liquid which Nature has enveloped in veils, this strange desire that assails all the races of mankind, in every climate and temperature, is most worthy to attract the attention of the philosophic observer.

I, among others, have pondered it, and I am tempted to place the craving for fermented liquors, which is unknown to animals, with anxiety regarding the future, which is likewise unknown to animals, and to regard both as distinctive attributes of the masterpiece of the last sublunary revolution.

> Jean-Anthelme Brillat-Savarin, *La Physiologie du Goût*, 1825

There is less logic but sincere belief in this passage of seventeenth-century correspondence.

Oh! That second Bottle is the Sincerest, Wisest, and most Impartial, Downright Friend we have; tells us truth of ourselves, and forces us to speak Truths of Others; banishes Flattery from our Tongues, and distrust from our Hearts; sets us above the mean Policy of Court Prudence; which makes us lie to one another all Day, for fear of being betrayed by each other at Night. And ... I believe, the errantest Vilain breathing, is honest as long as that Bottle lives.

> Earl of Rochester, Letter to Savile, *Familiar Letters*, 1685

Between the debater and the poet lies the relishing versifier:

It was my father's wine – alas!
  It was his chiefest bliss
To fill an old friend's evening glass
  With nectar such as this.
I think I have as warm a heart,
  As kind a friend as he;
Another bumper 'ere we part;
  Old wine, old wine for me!

In this we toasted William Pitt,
  Whom twenty now outshine;
O'er this we laughed at Canning's wit,
  Ere Hume's was thought as fine;
In this 'The King' – 'The Church' – 'The Laws'
  Have had their three times three;
Sound wine befits as sound a cause;
  Old wine, old wine for me!

In this when France in those long wars
  Was beaten black and blue,
We used to drink our troops and tars,
  Our Wellesley and Pellew.
Now things are changed, though Britain's fame
  May out of fashion be,
At least my wine remains the same;
  Old wine, old wine for me!

My neighbours, Robinson and Lamb,
  Drink French of last year's growth;
I'm sure, however they may sham,
  It disagrees with both;
I don't pretend to interfere;
  An Englishman is free;
But none of that cheap poison here:
  Old wine, old wine for me!

Some dozens lose, I must allow,
  Something of strength and hue;
And there are vacant spaces now
  To be filled up with new;
And there are cobwebs round the bins,
  Which some don't like to see;
If these are all my cellar's sins,
  Old wine, old wine for me!

Winthrop Mackworth Praed, *Poems,* 1864

Eventually, though, the gentler wisdoms must always prevail –

Lay hands suddenly on no man, neither be partaker of other men's sins: keep thyself pure.

Drink no longer water, but use a little wine for thy stomach's sake and thine often infirmities.

1 Timothy 5: 22, 23

> Fill ev'ry glass, for wine inspires us,
> And fires us
> With courage, love and joy.
> Women and wine should life employ.
> Is there aught else on earth desirous?

John Gay, *The Beggar's Opera*, 1728

The deeper understanding seems to lie often with the older thinkers.

> Then gan our hoste to laughen wonder loude
> And sayd: I see wel it is necessary
> Wher that we gon good drinke with us cary:
> For that wol turnen rancour and disese
> To accord and love, and many a wrong apese.
> O Bacchus, Bacchus, blessed be thy name.
> That so canst turnen ernest into game:
> Worship and thonke be to thy deitee.

Geoffrey Chaucer, *Canterbury Tales*, c. 1387

Give strong drink unto him that is ready to perish, and wine unto those that be of heavy hearts.

Let him drink and forget his poverty and remember his misery no more.

Ecclesiasticus 31: 6, 7

We may, as often, leave the last word with Shakespeare:

> Give me a bowl of wine.
> In this I bury all unkindness...

William Shakespeare, *Julius Caesar*, IV. iii.
1623

Origins

To go to the origins of wine is to recognize Noah as the first vigneron.

And Noah began to be an husbandman, and he planted a vineyard.

And he drank of the wine, and was drunken; and he was uncovered within his tent.

And Ham, the father of Canaan, saw the nakedness of his father, and told his two brethren without.

And Shem and Japheth took a garment, and laid it upon both their shoulders, and went backward, and covered the nakedness of their father; and their faces were backward, and they saw not their father's nakedness.

And Noah awoke from his wine, and knew what his younger son had done unto him.

Genesis 9: 20–4

The monastery view of the Ark's captain was tolerant – perhaps more tolerant than he deserved.

> There is no tre that growe
> On earthe, that I do knowe,
> More worthie praise, I trowe,
>   Then is the vyne:
> Whos grapes, as ye maye wede,
> Theire licoure forthe dothe shede,
> Whereof is made indede,
>   All our good wyne.
> And wyne ye maye trust me
> Causethe men for to be
> Merie, for so ye se
>   His nature is.

Then put aside all wrathe,
For David shewed us hathe,
Vinum letificat
  Cor hominis.

Wyne taken wth excesse,
As scripture dothe expres,
Causethe great hevines
  Unto the mynde.
But theie that take pleasure,
To drinke it wth measure,
No doute a great treasure
  They shall it finde.
Then voide you all sadnes,
Drinke youre wine with gladnes,
To take thought is madnes,
  And marke well this;
And put aside all wrathe,
For David showde us hathe,
Vinum letificat
  Cor hominis.

                Anonymous Monkish Rhyme

The seventeenth-century satirist was more acid.

So Noah, when he anchor'd safe on
The mountain's top, his lofty haven,
And all the passengers he bore
Were on the new world set ashore,
He made it next his chief design
To plant and propagate a vine,
Which since has overwhelm'd and drown'd
Far greater numbers, on dry ground,
Of wretched mankind, one by one,
Than all the flood before had done.

    Samuel Butler (1612–80), *Genuine Remains*, 1759

Here the last word may lie with a seventeenth-century divine:

Wine has drowned more men than the sea.

                  Thomas Fuller, 1608–61

The Other Side of the Glass

The case for wine is by no means one-sided and some fine minds and writing abilities have been applied to the other side of the question, including one of the greatest poets, certainly the greatest of all puritan poets.

Bacchus, that first from out the purple grape
Crushed the sweet poison of misused wine,
After the Tuscan mariners transformed,
Coasting the Tyrrhene shore, as the winds listed,
On Circe's island fell. (Who knows not Circe,
The daughter of the Sun, whose charmèd cup
Whoever tasted lost his upright shape,
And downward fell into a grovelling swine?)
This Nymph, that gazed upon his clustering locks,
With ivy berries wreathed, and his blithe youth,
Had by him, ere he parted thence, a son
Much like his father, but his mother more,
Whom therefore she brought up, and Comus
  named:
Who, ripe and frolic of his full-grown age,
Roving the Celtic and Iberian fields,
At last betakes him to this ominous wood,
And, in thick shelter of black shades imbowered,
Excels his mother at her mighty art;
Offering to every weary traveller
His orient liquor in a crystal glass,
To quench the drouth of Phœbus; which as they
  taste
(For most do taste through fond intemperate thirst),
Soon as the potion works, their human count'nance,
The express resemblance of the gods, is changed
Into some brutish form of wolf or bear,

An ounce or tiger, hog, or bearded goat,
All other parts remaining as they were.
And they, so perfect in their misery
Not once perceive their foul disfigurement,
But boast themselves more comely than before,
And all their friends and native home forget,
To roll with pleasure in a sensual sty.

John Milton, *Comus*, 1634

Another great Englishman was at pains to advise his
son against drinking, even if it was a case of 'Don't do
as I do, do as I say'.

Take especial care that you delight not in wine, for
there never was any man that came to honour or
preferment that loved it. For it transforms a man into
a beast, decays health, poisons the breath, destroys
natural heat, brings a man's stomach to an artificial
heat, deforms the face, rots the teeth, and to conclude
makes a man contemptible. Remember my words. It

were better for a man to be subject to any vice than to this. For all other vanities and sins are recovered, but a drunkard will never shake off the delight of beastliness. For the longer it possesses a man, the more he will delight in it; and the older he grows, the more he shall be subject to it. For it dulls the spirit and destroys the body as ivy does the old tree, or as the worm that ingenders in the kernel of the nut.

Take heed therefore that such a cureless canker pass not your youth, nor such a beastly infection your old age. For then shall all your life be but as the life of a beast, and after your death you shall only leave a shameful infamy to your posterity, who shall study to forget that such a one was their father.

St Augustine describes drunkenness in this manner:

'Drunkenness is a flattering devil, a sweet poison, a pleasant sin; which whosoever has, has not himself; which whosoever does commit, does not commit sin. but he himself is wholly sin.'

When Diogenes saw a house to be sold, whereof the owner was given to drink, I thought at the last, quoth Diogenes, he would spew out a whole house. *Sotebam, inquit, quod domum tandem evomeret.*

Sir Walter Ralegh (1552?–1618), *Advice to his Son*, 1632

Generally the writers have counselled moderation rather than abstention.

Good wine's the gift that God has given
To man alone beneath the heaven,
Of dance and song the genial sire,
Of friendship gay and soft desire;
Yet rule it with a tightened rein,
Nor moderate wisdom's rules disdain;
For when unchecked there's nought runs faster –
A useful slave, but cruel master.

Panyasis (c. 480 BC)

Here, too, we may turn to the Apocrypha:

Show not thy valiantness in wine; for wine has destroyed many.

The furnace proveth the edge by dipping; so doth wine the hearts of the proud by drunkenness. . . .

Wine measurably drunk and in season bringeth gladness of the heart, and cheerfulness of the mind:

But wine drunken with excess maketh bitterness of the mind, with brawling and quarrelling.

Drunkenness increaseth the rage of a fool till he offend: it diminisheth strength, and maketh wounds.

Rebuke not thy neighbour at the wine, and despise him not in his mirth: give him no despiteful words, and press not upon him with urging him (to drink).

Ecclesiasticus 31: 25–6, 28–31

The sternest of all prohibitions is that of the Nazarite.

He shall separate himself from the wine and strong drink, and shall drink no vinegar of wine, or vinegar of strong drink, neither shall he drink any liquor of grapes, nor eat moist grapes, or dried.

All the days of his separation shall he eat nothing that is made of the vine tree, from the kernels even to the husk.

Numbers 6: 3–4

The most thoughtful are the cautionary:

The first wrote, Wine is the strongest.

The second wrote, The King is strongest.

The third wrote, Women are strongest: but above all things Truth beareth away the victory.

Apocrypha, 1 Esdras: 3

Wine maketh merry: but money answereth all things.

Ecclesiastes 10: 19

One of the earliest of American interventions was

In the order named, these are the hardest to control: wine, women and song.

Franklin Adams (c. 1930)

[27]

If, though, we are looking for wisdom, – contentious wisdom – provocative wisdom, amusing wisdom, wisdom that made Boswell wriggle, we must turn to Dr Johnson, one who forsook drinking with a view to resuming and was none the happier for either.

He said that few people had intellectual resources sufficient to forgo the pleasures of wine. They could not otherwise contrive how to fill the interval between dinner and supper.

*   *   *

Wine makes a man better pleased with himself; I do not say that it makes him more pleasing to others.

*   *   *

Talking of the effects of drinking, he said, 'Drinking may be practised with great prudence; a man who exposes himself when he is intoxicated has not the art of getting drunk; a sober man who happens occasionally to get drunk, readily enough goes into a new company, which a man who has been drinking should never do. Such a man will undertake anything: he is without skill in inebriation. I used to slink home when I had drunk too much. A man accustomed to self-examination will be conscious when he is drunk, though an habitual drunkard will not be conscious of it. I knew a physician who for twenty years was not sober; yet in a pamphlet, which he wrote upon fevers, he appealed to Garrick and me for his vindication from a charge of drunkenness. A bookseller (naming him) who got a large fortune by trade, was so habitually and equably drunk, that his most intimate friends never perceived that he was more sober at one time than another.'

*   *   *

As we drove back to Ashbourne, Dr Johnson recommended to me, as he had often done, to drink water only: 'For (said he) you are then sure not to get drunk;

whereas if you drink wine you are never sure.' I said, drinking wine was a pleasure which I was unwilling to give up. 'Why, Sir, (said he), there is no doubt that not to drink wine is a great deduction from life; but it may be necessary.' He however owned, that in his opinion a free use of wine did not shorten life; and said, he would not give less for the life of a certain Scotch Lord (whom he named) celebrated for hard drinking, than for that of a sober man. 'But stay, (said he with his usual intelligence, and accuracy of inquiry), does it take much wine to make him drunk?' I answered, 'A great deal either of wine or strong punch' – 'Then, (said he) that is the worse.' I presume to illustrate my friend's observation thus: 'A fortress which soon surrenders has its walls less shattered, than when a long and obstinate resistance is made.'

*   *   *

Talking of drinking wine, he said, 'I did not leave off wine because I could not bear it: I have drunk three bottles of port without being the worse for it. University College has witnessed this.' BOSWELL: 'Why, then, Sir, did you leave it off?' JOHNSON: 'Why, Sir, because it is so much better for a man to be sure that he is never to be intoxicated, never to lose the power over himself. I shall not begin to drink wine again until I grow old, and want it.' BOSWELL: 'I think, Sir, you once said to me, that not to drink wine was a great deduction from life.' JOHNSON: 'It is a diminution of pleasure, to be sure; but I do not say a diminution of happiness. There is more happiness in being rational.' BOSWELL: 'But if we could have pleasure always, should not we be happy? The greatest part of men would compound for pleasure.' JOHNSON: 'Supposing we could have pleasure always, an intellectual man would not compound for it. The greatest part of men would compound, because the greatest part of men are gross.' BOSWELL: 'I allow there may be greater pleasure than from wine. I have had more pleasure from your conversation. I have indeed; I assure you I have.' JOHNSON: 'When we talk of pleasure, we mean sensual pleasure. When a man says he had pleasure with a woman, he does not mean conversation, but something of a very different nature. Philosophers tell you, that pleasure is *contrary* to happiness. Gross men prefer animal pleasure. So there are men who have preferred living among savages. Now what a wretch must he be, who is content with such conversation as can be had among savages! You may remember an officer at Fort Augustus, who had served in America, told us of a woman whom they were obliged to *bind*, in order to get her back from savage life.' BOSWELL: 'She must have been an animal, a beast.' JOHNSON: 'Sir, she was a speaking cat.'

James Boswell, *Life of Johnson*, 1791

The gloomy but probably accurate prophesy from a physician two hundred years earlier:

Drink wine and have gout; drink none and have the gout.

Dr Thomas Coggan (fl. 1590)

While three centuries later came

Empty wine bottles have a bad opinion of women.

Ambrose Bierce (1842–1914)

On the limitations of temperance, the joint Elizabethan playwrights were content to generalize:

I love good wine
As I love health and joy of heart, but temperately.

Beaumont and Fletcher

So, too, was the classical poet of elegant love.

I own, I think of wine the moderate use
More suits the sex and sooner finds excuse.
It warms the blood, adds lustre to the eyes,
And Wine and Love have ever been allies;

But carefully from all intemperance keep,
Nor drink till you see double, lisp, or sleep.

Ovid (c. 3 BC)

Precision has not always been lacking. Indeed, there has been an odd, widely distributed degree of unanimity on the desirable number of drinks. It first seems to have been stated in the second century.

Three cups of wine a prudent man may take:
The first of them for constitution sake;
The second, to the girl he loves the best;
The third and last, to lull him to his rest –
Then home to bed. But, if a fourth he pours,
That is the cup of folly, and not ours.
Loud noisy talking on the fifth attends;
The sixth breeds feuds, and falling out of friends;
Seven beget blows, and faces stained with gore;
Eight, and the watch patrole breaks ope' the door;
Mad with the ninth, another cup goes round,
And the swilled sot drops senseless on the ground.

Athenaeus, *Deipnosophistai, c.* AD 200

Then, half a millennium later, there was confirmation from China:

Three cups and one can perfectly understand the Great Tao.

Li T'ai Po, *c.* AD 740

There is undated agreement from a nearby source:

At the first cup the man drinks wine; at the second cup wine drinks wine; at the third cup wine drinks the man.

Japanese proverb

No doubt it all hinges upon the size of the glass or cup, and to round off a strangely assorted consensus we may call in a Metaphysical poet –

Drink not the third glass, which thou
   canst not tame,
When once it is within thee.

George Herbert, 'The Church-porch', *The
Temple*, 1634

*As the last word was left to Shakespeare in praise of
wine, so he may have the last two here:*

Great men should drink with harness on their
throats.

Timon of Athens I. ii., 1623

Oh thou invisible spirit of wine! If thou hast no
name to be known by, let us call thee devil!

Othello, II. iii., 1622

The World of Wines

The variety of wine is infinite. In Bordeaux alone over 4,000 'principal' vineyards are listed, each of which produces a wine marginally different from its neighbour's because of the variation of the soils, micro-climates, the mixture of grapes, and the vigneron's own personal style of making. Unlike the students of Cocks et Feret – the encyclopaedia of Bordeaux wines – the people of the rest of the world are content with fewer varieties. Although the English do not produce any measurable quantity of wine, they enjoy world variety uninhibited by regional or local loyalties, as that perceptive wine drinker, Byron observed.

> An English autumn, though it hath no vines
>   Blushing with Bacchant coronals along
> The paths, o'er which the far festoon entwines
>   The red grape in the sunny lands of song,
> Hath yet a purchased choice of choicest wines;
>   The claret light and the Madeira strong.
> If Britain mourn her bleakness, we can tell her,
> The very best of vineyards is the cellar.

Lord Byron, *Don Juan*, 1819–20

Earlier English advice was not specific in naming the wine, but in demanding of it certain characteristics.

Choose your wine after this sort; it must be fragrant and redolent, having a good odour and flavour in the nose; it must sprinkle in the cup when it is drawn or put out of the pot into the cup; it must be cold and pleasant in the mouth; and it must be strong and subtle of substance. And then moderately drunken it doth quicken a man's wits, it doth comfort the heart, it doth scour the liver; specially, if it be white wine, it doth rejoice all the powers of man, and doth nourish them; it doth engender good blood, it doth comfort and doth nourish the brain and all the body, and it resolveth fleume; it engendereth heat, and it is good against heaviness and pensifulness; it is full of agility; wherefore it is medicinable, specially white wine, for it doth mundify and cleanse wounds and sores.

Andrew Boorde, *Dyetary*, 1562

Until at least recent times it seems to have been accepted that the great appreciators of wine were men. One lady, though – French, of course – grew up in deep critical appreciation.

I was very well brought up. As convincing proof of such a categorical assertion, let me say that when I was barely three years of age my father, who believed in gentle and progressive methods, gave me a full liqueur glass of a reddish-brown wine sent to him from his native Southern France; the Muscat Wine of Frontignan.

It was like a sun-stroke, or love at first sight, or the sudden realization of a nervous system; this consecration rendered me a worthy disciple of Wine for ever afterwards. A little later, I learnt to quaff my glass of mulled wine, aromatic, with cinnamon and lemon, to a dinner of boiled chestnuts. At the age when one can barely read I was spelling out, drop by drop, red Burgundies, old and light, and dazzling Yquems. Champagne passed in its turn, a murmur of foam, leaping pearls of air, across birthday dinners and first communion festivities: with it came grey Puisaye truffles ... A fine lesson from which I acquired familiar and discreet knowledge of wine, not swallowed greedily, but measured out into narrow glasses, absorbed in mouthfuls with long spaces in between and carefully reflected upon.

It was between my eleventh and my fifteenth years that this beautiful educational programme was completed. My mother feared that, as I grew older, I should become anaemic. One by one, she unearthed from their dry sand some bottles which were ageing beneath our house in a cellar – it is, thank Heavens! still intact – carved out of the granite itself. Whenever I think about it, I envy the little brat who was so privileged. To accompany my modest provisions on my return to school – a cutlet, the drumstick of a chicken, or one of those hard cheeses that are matured beneath wood-cinders and which one breaks into splinters with a blow from one's fist like a pane of glass – I had Château-Larose, Château-Lafite, Chambertin and Corton which had escaped the Prussians in 1860. Certain of the wines had perished and were pale and smelt faintly of dead roses; they rested in a bed of tannin which dyed the bottles deeply; but most of them kept their fine fire, strength and vigour. What delightful times those were! I drained the cream of the paternal cellar, glass by glass, delicately ... My mother recorked the open bottles and contemplated the glory of the French vintages on my colouring cheeks.

How lucky are the children who do not distend their stomachs with great draughts of artificially reddened wine at meals! How well advised are the parents who dole out to their offspring an inch of pure wine – meaning 'pure' in the highest sense of the word – and teach them that: 'When it is not mealtime, you have the pump, the tap, the springs and filters. Water is for thirst! Wine is, according to its quality and its flavour, a necessary tonic, a luxury or a tribute paid to food.'

It is not also a nourishment? What lovely times those were when the natives of my village in Lower Burgundy would gather around a bottle clad in dust and silky cobwebs and kiss their fingers in the air to it, exclaiming – even before tasting it – 'Nectar!' Do you not admit, then, that in telling you about wine here I am speaking about what I know? It is not a little thing to have learnt contempt, at an early age, both for those who drink no wine and those who drink too much.

Colette, *Prisons et Paradis*, 1966

There exists much serious advice on tasting but none more humorously observant than this:

It takes twenty years of hard work to develop a discriminating palate for wine. Having been brought up on gin and beer and also being poor, I certainly will never know much more than that wine is good. But while working at this book I must have tasted wines a score of times in the company of experts. Before the end I had developed a technique which deceived the most critical *Maître de chai* or *Chef de caves*. For what they are worth I will pass on my notes. (A *chai*, by the way, is a ground-level cellar where barrels are kept; a *cave* is an underground cellar.)

The first rule is to say nothing. Actions and expressions are more significant and much safer than words. A mistake most amateurs make at first is to behave as if they were being judged by the wine and by the company. That may be true. But behave as if you were doing the interviewing – with dignity, courtesy, keen interest, and decision.

When the wine-glass is handed to you, do not take it by the stem but by the base, between forefinger and thumb. Bow to the man who gives it to you. Hold the glass up to the light, peer at it, and nod your head. Then stand for twenty seconds at least, frowning slightly and swilling the wine round and round in the glass. You must not spill it, of course, but it is most impressive if you can learn – with a glass of water in your bedroom – to make it swish round just below the rim, as fast as a motor-cyclist on the wall of death. Having done this, you study your wine-glass again, this time with the expression you might wear while reading small type. What you are looking at is the speed or slowness with which the last of the wine drains down the sides of the glass.

Then swish it round again and immediately afterwards cup your two hands about the bowl and bury your nose in it as if you were inhaling something for a cold. When you lift your face again the fumes of the wine, the bouquet at the back of your nose, will of their own accord have given you the right expression. But you may accentuate the effect by throwing up your eyes and then bowing your head. After that, swish the wine round the glass, frowning thoughtfully.

Now take a mouthful. A mistake most novices fall into is to take a sip, which gives them away at once. You must take a great hungry gulp of wine. But you don't swallow it, of course. You chew it. You push it forward through your teeth with your tongue and suck it up to the back-door of your nose. If the *Maître de chai* is watching you at this time, as he certainly will be, make sure that all your facial muscles are working. But look at nobody yourself. Your eyes must be far away in the dim recesses of the cellar.

You should practise this chewing, for you must be able to keep it up for a long time without swallowing, which is not easy. Your face works more and more strongly. You have now appeared to appreciate the wine with all your sensory nerves. You have reached your decision. The moment of climax has come.

The climax is the spit. Again and again I have seen a good performance ruined by the spit. It is disastrous to bend down in a corner and merely open your mouth. It is little better to purse your lips as if you were getting rid of a cherry stone.

You have reached your decision, remember; so your spit must underline it. It must be bold and emphatic as an exclamation mark. The way to do it is to draw your shut lips wide as if you were about to whistle for a taxi, and with a tremendous flick of the tongue send the stuff jetting out so that it strikes the floor like a fist banged on a table. Then look round at everybody happily and proudly, because you have been allowed to share in a tremendous secret.

If you are unable to perfect the spit, then swallow. But don't do it steadily. Do it as if carried away by passion, and afterwards slap your chest gaily to

emphasize your independence. But there are disadvantages in swallowing if there are many wines to taste during the morning. There are always disadvantages about being carried away by passion.

All this, you notice, has been done without a word. Only at the moment of leaving the cellar need you speak. You step impulsively up to the *Maître de chai* and wring his hand and mutter, '*Merci, Maître, merci, merci,*' then hurry out of doors.

In the sunlight there may be discussion about the wines. This need not alarm you, for your sense of hearing has been as busy as the rest and you have probably overheard some safe opinions. '*Très souple*' is generally a safe one. But unless asked a direct question, it is best to maintain a sphinx-like silence, smiling knowingly at the whole world from half-shut eyes.

J. M. Scott, *Vineyards of France*, 1950

The British capacity to learn the subject became part of their civilization as one observant American was quick to recognize.

The Government of the world I live in was not framed, like that of Britain, in after-dinner conversations over the wine.

Henry Thoreau, *Walden*, 1854

[38]

It must always be a matter of preference, if not of bias, to place wines in order. We may, though, without arousing suspicion, begin with the aperitifs. Earliest in date, surely, sherry – the sherris sack not known in the England of Falstaff's day, but put into his mouth by Shakespeare as the instrument of his own enthusiasm.

'I would you had the wit: 'twere better than a dukedom. Good faith, this same young sober-blooded boy doth not love me; nor a man cannot make him laugh; but that's no marvel, he drinks no wine. There's never none of these demure boys come to any proof; for thin drink doth so over-cool their blood, and making many fish meals, that they fall into a kind of male green-sickness; and then, when they marry, they get wenches: they are generally fools and cowards; which some of us should be too, but for inflammation. A good sherry-sack hath a two-fold operation in it. It ascends me into the brain; dries me there all the foolish and dull and crudy vapours which environ it; it makes it apprehensive, quick, forgetive, full of nimble, fiery and delectable shapes; which delivered over to the voice, the tongue, which is the birth, becomes excellent wit. The second property of your excellent sherris is, the warming of the blood; which before, cold and settled, left the liver white and pale, which is the badge of pusillanimity and cowardice; but the sherris warms it and makes it course from the inwards to parts extreme: it illumineth the face, which as a beacon gives warning to all the rest of this little kingdom, man, to arm; and then the vital commoners and inland spirits muster me all to their captain, the heart, who, great and puffed up with this retinue, doth any deed of courage; and this value comes of sherris. So that skill in the weapon is nothing without sack, for that sets it a-work; and learning a mere hoard of gold kept by the devil, till sack commences it and sets it in act and use. Hereof comes it that Prince Harry is valiant; for the cold blood he did naturally inherit of his father, he hath, like lean, sterile, and bare land, manured, husbanded and tilled with such excellent endeavour of drinking good and good store of fertile sherris, that he is become very hot and valiant. If I had a thousand sons, the first humane principle I should teach them would be, to forswear thin potations and to addict themselves to sack.'

William Shakespeare, *Henry IV, Part 2*, IV. iii., 1600

Nor was Shakespeare alone in his enthusiasm –

I shall never forget the astonishment of a servant I had recommended to him. On entering his service, John made his appearance as Fiennes was going out to dinner, and asked his new master if he had any orders. He received the following answer – 'Place two bottles of sherry by my bedside, and call me the day after tomorrow.'

Captain R. H. Gronow, *Reminiscences*, 1861

That eminent scholar of wine, George Saintsbury, agreed on its attraction.

The extraordinary *adaptableness* of sherry may deserve a few words. It does, perhaps, lend itself too freely to 'mixtures'. 'Sherry cobbler' is indeed a most excellent drink. I was taught to make it when I was an undergraduate by no less a person than the late 'Father' Stanton, who was as good a fellow as he was a godly man; and the preliminary process of 'cataracting' the wine and the ice and the lemon from two properly handled and not pusillanimously approximated soda-water tumblers is a beautiful and noble occupation.

In fact the unusual range of alcoholic strength, and the great diversity of flavour and body in the different sherries make dilution almost unnecessary, except for persons who must have 'long drinks'. Manzanilla will carry you nearly through dinner, and others of the lighter class will go all through, though they may not

be drinkable in quite such volume. I once even attempted a fully graded *menu* and wine-list with sherry
only to fill the latter – a 'sherry dinner' to match the
claret feasts often given by lovers of Gascon wine. It
was before I began to keep such documents, and so
I am not quite certain of the details. But if I were
reconstructing such an entertainment now, and had
the wherewithal as I once had, I should arrange it
somewhat thus: Manzanilla with oysters; Montilla with
soup and fish; an Amontillado with entrées and roast;
an Amoroso or some such wine with sweets; and for
after dinner, the oldest and brownest of 'old browns', say
Brown Bristol Milk, which in its turn doubly suggests
a finish to this notice. The very darkest sherry I ever
possessed, indeed that I ever tasted or saw, was an
1870 wine specially yclept 'Caveza', which I bought
when it was more than twenty years old, and of which
I still had some when it was over forty. It was not an
absolutely first-class wine, but good enough, and remarkable for its extraordinary, and not easily describ-
able colour – almost black except against the light.
This brought about an incident slightly comic. I was
giving a dinner-party in the early nineties, and a
decanter of this wine was put on the table. Whereupon
one of my guests (a medical man not quite so amply
possessed of convivial amiability as some others of the
faculty) proceeded positively to lose his temper over it.
'It was not sherry; it couldn't be sherry; there never
was sherry of that colour; it must be queer-coloured
port mislabelled.' Neither his host's assurances, nor
those of his fellow guests, nor appeal to his own
taste and smell would satisfy him; and things were
getting almost unpleasant when I managed to turn
the conversation.

George Saintsbury, *Notes on a Cellar Book*, 1920

Disputing the place of the leading aperitif with sherry
is the historically younger champagne, a drink not only

*appetizing and refreshing, but, in the imagination of
its drinkers at all levels, romantic.*

> Give me Champagne and fill it to the brim,
> I'll toast in bumpers ev'ry lovely limb;
> I challenge all the heroes of the skies
> To show a goddess with a Craven's eyes.
> Why then averse to love? Ah, leave disdain,
> Discard thy fickle undeserving swain,
> and pledge thy lover in the brisk Champaign.

> Lord Chesterfield, *Witticisms,* 1773

*On the popular level in Britain, of course, it became
the wine of the variety halls:*

> For Champagne Charlie is my name
> Champagne Charlie is my name,
> Good for any game at night, my boys,
> Good for any game at night, my boys,
> For Champagne Charlie is my name,
> Champagne Charlie is my name,
> Good for any game at night, my boys,
> Who'll come and join me in a spree?

> From Coffee and from Supper Rooms,
> From Poplar to Pall Mall,
> The girls on seeing me, exclaim
> 'Oh, what a Champagne Swell!'
> The notion 'tis of everyone
> If 'twere not for my name,
> And causing so much to be drunk,
> They'd never make Champagne.

> Chorus: For Champagne Charlie is my
> name, etc.

> Some epicures like Burgundy,
> Hock, Claret, and Moselle,
> But Moet's vintage only
> Satisfies this Champagne swell.

What matter if to bed I go
Dull head and muddled thick,
A bottle in the morning
Sets me right then very quick.

> Chorus: For Champagne Charlie is my
> name, etc.

Perhaps you fancy what I say
Is nothing else but chaff,
And only done, like other songs
To merely raise a laugh.
To prove that I am not in jest,
Each man a bottle of Cham.
I'll stand fizz round, yes that I will,
And stand it like a lamb.

> Chorus: For Champagne Charlie, etc.

George Leybourne, nineteenth-century music-hall
performer

*The French must be allowed their splendidly imagin-
ative opinion – imaginative even in a historian –*

In this naïve and shrewd champagne, ends the long
line which we have followed, from Languedoc and
Provence, by Burgundy and Lyons; in this vinous
and literary zone the spirit of man has continually
prospered in clarity and sobriety.

We may distinguish three degrees, the fiery and
impetuous Midi, the rhetorical eloquence of Burgundy,
and the grace and irony of Champagne. This is the
final flowering of the French spirit and the most
delicate.

On these white plains, on these meagre hills, ripens
the wine of northern France full of sallies and caprices.
It owes little to the earth, it is the fruit of labour.

Jules Michelet (1798–1874)

or, through a poet most admirably translated.

[43]

Sparkling wine
Chloris, Aegle pouring with their hand
A wine of Ay whose froth presses
In the bottle with increasing force,

Shoots out the cork like lightning;
It leaps and hits the ceiling.
This fresh wine with bubbling froth
Is the very image of our France.

Voltaire (1694–1778), 'Champagne'

A thoughtful, if not always – at least to the modern mind – flattering opinion comes from the nineteenth century when many wines were not quite what they should have been.

Another word should be said to men of moderate means about that same champagne. It is actually one of the cheapest of wines, and there is no wine, out of which, to speak commercially, you get your returns so directly. The popping, and fizzing, and agreeable nervous hurry in pouring and drinking, give it a prestige and an extra importance – it makes twice the appearance, has twice the effect, and doesn't cost you more than a bottle of your steady, old, brown sherry, which has gathered on his head the interest of accumulated years in your cellar. When people have had plenty of champagne they fancy they have been treated liberally. If you wish to save, save upon your hocks, Sauternes, and Moselles, which count for nothing, but disappear down careless throats like so much toast and water.

I have made this remark about champagne. All men of the world say they don't care for it; all gourmands swear and vow that they prefer Sillery a thousand times to sparkling, but look round the table and behold! We all somehow drink it. All who say they like the Sillery will be found drinking the sparkling. Yes, beloved sparkler, you are an artificial, barley-sugared, brandied beverage, according to the dicta of connoisseurs. You are universally sneered at, and said to have no good in you. But console yourself, you are universally drunken – you are the wine of the world – you are the liquor in whose bubbles lies the greatest amount of the sparkle of good spirits. May I die but I will not be ashamed to proclaim my love for you! You have given me much pleasure, and never any pain – you have stood by me in many hard moments, and cheered me in many dull ones – you have whipped up many flagging thoughts, and dissipated many that were gloomy – you have made me hope, ay, and forget. Ought a man to disown such a friend?

Incomparably the best champagne I know is to be found in England. It is the most doctored, the most brandied, the most barley-sugared, the most *winy* wine in the world. As such let us hail, and honour, and love it.

W. M. Thackeray (1811–63), *Barmecide Banquets*

[45]

A major observer, interpreter, and historian of champagne is an Englishman, who worked long in the trade and in France.

The process by which wine is put through a double fermentation – one in an open receptacle, the other in an hermetically sealed bottle – is known as the *méthode champenoise*. The law of France insists that champagne must be made according to this method. In other parts of the country wine-makers are at perfect liberty to make sparkling wine in whatever way they wish, but in no circumstances may they call it champagne; if, however, the sparkling wine was made by the *méthode champenoise*, that fact may be mentioned on the label.

Many people who have been swigging champagne for a lifetime are unaware of the fact that the wine is made predominantly from the juice of red grapes. This apparent anomaly is rendered possible because the actual juice of the red grapes grown in the winefield, like the juice of most red grapes, is white, the pigmentation being in the skin. By pressing the red grapes in a special manner and removing the skins immediately after the pressing, juice which has hardly a trace of red in it is obtained. This juice imparts a 'body', an importance, one might say, to champagne which the juice of white grapes alone can seldom give it. But if it were all 'body', all importance, champagne would not be champagne. It is the addition of a judicious quantity – the ideal proportion is generally about one-third – of the juice of the white grapes grown in the winefield that produces, in conjunction with 'body', the fragrance, the brightness of champagne.

The art of blending champagne, however, is not just a matter of choosing the right proportion of juice derived from red and white grapes; selecting the vineyards from which the grapes come is of equal importance. A bottle of the best champagne may contain the juice of fifteen different vineyards, and some excellent champagnes are composed of juice obtained from over thirty different vineyards.

Now this is matter to reflect upon, because the wine of very great vineyards in other winefields is never blended ... Which leads to the question: why do the Champenois make such extensive use of blending when makers of other great wines do not?

They do so for two good reasons. The first is simply that long experience has proved that as a general rule a far finer champagne is achieved from a blending of the produce of several vineyards than from that of a single red-grape one and a single white-grape one.

The other reason has to do with the northern climate of the Falaises. It would cause a great deal of disappointment in the world if, as a result of a series of calamities that befell the crop, the Champenois announced, 'We're awfully sorry, but we're making no champagne this year, and probably none next year either'. As it is, they avoid having to do so by making two distinct types of blend.

Vintage champagne is a blend of the wines of one exceptionally good year. The year in question (the year the grapes were picked) is indicated on the label. The amount of vintage champagne made is never very great, because, even in an exceptionally good year, a large proportion of that year's wine is taken down to the cellars and stored there until such time as it is needed to make non-vintage champagne. For non-vintage champagne is a blend not only of the wines of different vineyards but of different years as well. Thanks to this arrangement, no matter what sort of disaster may have befallen the vines in the previous spring, summer or autumn, the champagne-maker always has at his disposal, deep in his cellars, reserves of wine of preceding years which he can blend and bottle.

Patrick Forbes, *Champagne*, 1967

He is sound, too, on the people of champagne – the Champenoises:

The ownership of the vineyards in the Champagne district is split between a greater number of people than is the case in any of the other great French winefields. There are no less than 16,250 proprietors of the 44,478 acres planted with vines. Only 14 per cent of the vineyards (6,000 acres) belong to the *négociants en vin de champagne*; several champagne firms whose names are known throughout the civilized world do not own a single vine.

Two factors are responsible for this extraordinary state of affairs. One is the clause in the Code Napoléon concerning inheritance, which stipulates that most of a deceased person's property must be divided equally between his progeny. The other is the reluctance of the Champenois to sell a square inch of vineyard if they can possibly help it.

Indeed, in view of the tenacity with which the Champenois cling to their vineyards, what is surprising is that the ownership of the holdings is not still further split up, and that the *négociants* have succeeded in acquiring as much of the winefield as they have. For most of the big Houses would nowadays much prefer to own more vineyards – more high-class vineyards especially – and work them themselves with salaried workers, rather than, as they have to now, buy the majority of the grapes they need from the small proprietors.

As there are over 16,250 vineyard proprietors in the Champagne district, the size of the majority of the holdings is naturally exceptionally small. 1,988 cover less than a quarter of an acre. There are believed to be only nine holdings in the whole region that cover an area of more than 123 acres.

Remarkable as the figures are, they do not show something even more remarkable still: the minute size of the majority of the individual plots of vines. Partly as a result of the Code Napoléon and partly because everyone who makes champagne prefers to have several parcels of vines rather than one big one, in order to

have a choice of grapes for the *cuvée*, the average champagne vineyard is probably about the area of a soccer field; some are no bigger than tennis-courts. Stones, carved with initials of the proprietor, indicate the boundaries of the respective properties and are often encountered every ten yards or so.

Patrick Forbes, *Champagne*, 1967

Some of the salutes to champagne have lost the name of their composers in their progress through the music-halls of the nineteenth-century, such as:

> The way I gained my title's
> By a hobby which I've got
> Of never letting others pay
> However long the shot;
> Whoever drinks at my expense
> Are treated all the same,
> From Dukes and Lords, to cabmen down,
> I make them drink Champagne.

and another:

> Here's to champagne the drink divine
> That makes us forget our troubles;
> It's made of a dollar's worth of wine
> And three dollars' worth of bubbles.

But a name is put to this impression of the famous gambling club:

> While Champagne in close array,
> Pride of Reims and Epernay,
> Not in bottles but in dozens,
> (Think of that, ye country cousins!)
> Stood, of every growth and price,
> Peeping forth its tubs of ice.

Henry Luttrell, 'Crockford's House', 1827

And still within the same period –

> If ever you've seen a party
> Relieved of the presence of Ned,
> How instantly joyous and hearty
> They've grown when the damper was fled.
> You may guess what a gay piece of work,
> What delight to Champagne it must be,
> To get rid of its bore of a cork,
> And come sparkling to you, love, and me.

Thomas Moore (1779–1852), 'Illustrations of a Bore'

Since there was no true champagne in Shakespeare's day, the last word on it may be left with the poet of wine:

> ... champagne with foaming whirls,
> As white as Cleopatra's melted pearls.

> The evaporation of a joyous day
> Is like the last glass of champagne, without
> The foam which made its virgin bumper gay ...

Lord Byron, *Don Juan*, Cantos XV and XVI, 1819–24

Once the drinker approaches the question of red wine, he becomes involved in the recurrent debate, if not conflict, between the claret of Bordeaux and the red of Burgundy.

'Claret is king.'
   'Not so! For me
The king of wines is Burgundy,
The puissant and royal wine.
That dukes of the Burgundian line
Drank once in Dijon.'
   'How you gloat
On treasures of your Golden Côte,
Your Nuits, your Beaune! Therein we see,
I grant you, high nobility,
But balance, *nuance,* these are found
On Bordelais, not Burgundian ground.
Claret is king.'
   'What can you see
In Claret's puny subtlety
To rival Bourgogne's *robe,* its strong
Savour of sun and vintage song?
Bourgogne is king.'
   'Nonsense! Bordeaux!'
'A certain courtesy we owe
In vinous argument.'
   'Agreed.'
'Then let us give each wine its meed,
Which compromise I take to mean
That one is king, the other queen.
You differ?'
   'Rather I divine
A Dual Monarchy of Wine.'

                   Eric Chilman, *Wine and Food*

*To begin alphabetically with Bordeaux is also to recall
one immortal passage:*

I never drink above three glasses of wine, and never
any spirits and water; though, by the by, the other day
Woodhouse took me to his coffee-house, and ordered a
bottle of claret. How I like claret! When I can get
claret, I must drink it. 'Tis the only palate affair that
I am at all sensual in. Would it not be a good spec.
to send you some vine-roots? Could it be done? I'll

inquire. If you could make some wine like claret, to
drink on summer evenings in an arbour! It fills one's
mouth with a gushing freshness, then goes down cool
and feverless; then, you do not feel it quarrelling with
one's liver. No; 'tis rather a peace-maker, and lies as
quiet as it did in the grape. Then it is as fragrant as
the Queen Bee, and the more ethereal part mounts into
the brain, not assaulting the cerebral apartments, like
a bully looking for his trull, and hurrying from door
to door, bouncing against the wainscot, but rather
walks like Aladdin about his enchanted palace, so
gently that you do not feel his step. Other wines of
a heavy and spirituous nature transform a man into
a Silenus, this makes him a Hermes, and gives a woman
the soul and immortality of an Ariadne, for whom
Bacchus always kept a good cellar of claret, and even
of that he never could persuade her to take above two
cups. I said this same claret is the only palate-passion
I have; I forgot game; I must plead guilty to the
breast of a partridge, the back of a hare, the back-bone
of a grouse, the wing and side of a pheasant, and a
wood-cock *passim*.

> John Keats, Letter to George and Georgiana Keats
> in America, February 1819

*One considerable poem called simply 'Wine' eventually
makes its way specifically to claret:*

The stairs' ascent now gained, our guard unbars
The door of spacious room, and creaking chairs
(To ear offensive) round the table sets,
We sit, when thus his florid speech begins:
Name, sirs, the wine that most invites you, taste
Champagne or burgundy, or Florence pure, or hock,
    antique,
Of Lisbon new or old, Bordeaux, or neat French
    white, or Alicante:
For Bordeaux we with voice unanimous
Declare, (such sympathy's in boon compeers.)
He quits the room alert but soon returns,

One hand capacious glittering vessels bore
Resplendent, the other with a grasp secure,
A bottle (mighty charge) upstaid, full fraught
With goodly wine, he with extended hand
Raised high, pours forth the sanguine frothy juice,
Or spread with bubbles, dissipated soon:
We straight to our arms repair, experienced chiefs;
Now glasses clash with glasses, (charming sound),
Of happiness terrestrial, and the source
Whence human pleasures flow, sing heavenly muse
Of sparkling juices, of the enlivening grape
Whose quickening taste adds vigour to the soul,
Whose sovereign power revives decaying nature
And thaws the frozen blood of hoary age
A kindly warmth defusing, youthful fires
Guild his dim eyes, and paint with ruddy hue
His wrizzled visage, ghastly wan before:
Cordial restorer to mortal man
With copious hand by bounteous gods bestowed.

John Gay, 'Wine', 1708

*The most encyclopaedic wine writer of the present time,
in a general review of Bordeaux wines, tells the most
charming claret story with characteristic style.*

For Montrose I have a special weakness. The château
belongs to Madame Charmolüe, but it is her son and
his wife who are always there, and the wine today is
his responsibility. The château is a small Victorian
house, very mildly assuming the airs of a great proprietor. From its windows you can see the vines sloping
away in the distance down to the broad brown Gironde.

Montrose always seems to me to have a touch of
lovely sweetness, a trace of some very generous and
kindly quality, only partly concealed by the considerable power of a great and classic wine. No doubt
memories have coloured it in my mind, for it was here
that, on my first visit, M. Charmolüe quietly put half
a dozen bottles of his wine in the back of my car
before I drove away. The next weekend I was on my

own up in the lovely remote country of the Dordogne, staying and eating my evening meal at a *routiers* café. I drank one of the bottles of Montrose with my dinner, and was so happy with it that I went out to the car to get the other five and gave them (it makes me sound mad) to the lorry-drivers who were in the café eating their stew. They evidently thought I was mad, too; they had probably never drunk a château-bottled second-growth claret before. In any case, they raised their glasses politely, and were about to empty them, when they stopped in mid-swallow. A look of immense pleasure, the expression of a true connoisseur face to face with a masterpiece, came over their faces. It was the scent of the wine, the clean, sweet, exquisite breath of autumn ripeness, which held them rapt. I do not think I exaggerate. It was a wonderful sight to see those great *onze-degrés* men, those pushers of gigantic trucks and trailers, breathing in the bouquet of a wine which spoke straight to them.

Hugh Johnson, *Wine*, 1966

The most erudite of English wine scholars has paid particular and revealing attention to Bordeaux wine and its history.

In 1401 King Henry IV imposed the condition on the merchants in 'enemy-held territories' that they must send one *tonneau* of corn for every two *tonneaux* of wine. As the merchants had nowhere else to dispose of their wine, they had no option but to comply.

If wine was France's chief medieval export, it was also England's largest import, and although separate statistics for Gascon wine imports are rare, most French wine to be found in England then was from Gascony. At its height in the fourteenth century it represented 31 per cent of our imports, compared with 1 per cent today. Indeed on *per capita* basis the amount of Gascon wine imported into England in the early fourteenth century has never been equalled. Over 20,000 tuns came in annually, representing between a quarter and a fifth of Bordeaux exports. Translated into hectolitres this amounted to 180,000. Yet in so recent a year as 1978 the total quantity of Bordeaux wines exported to Britain was no more than 176,000 hl. Early in the fourteenth century the Bordelais were exporting from Bordeaux, Libourne and the smaller Gironde ports as much as 90,000–100,000 *tonneaux* a year. . . .

What good customers the English kings were to their wine merchants is shown by the fact that in the early fourteenth century the normal 'annual order' given by the royal butler for the use of the court varied from 1,000–2,000 *tonneaux*; and to celebrate his marriage with Isabella of France in January 1308, Edward II ordered 1,000 *tonneaux*. By modern reckoning this would have produced something like 1,152,000 bottles. Quite a wedding!

Edmund Penning-Rowsell, *The Wines of Bordeaux*,
1969

His sensibility, though, lures him out beyond his historical brief to deal with another aspect of the Medoc.

It is appropriate to pass to Mouton's positive contribution to the relation between art and wine: the *Musée du Vin*. This remarkable collection, open since 1962 to all who care to apply in advance to the secretary of the château, is assembled in a former cellar, lying between the *cuvier* and the other *chais*. Every object, whether a fourteenth-century BC Mycenaean *krater*; a James II silver cup; a series of fifteenth-century Rhine

Valley tapestries, on work in the vineyard, reunited here after being as far afield as the U.S.A. and Italy; a Picasso gouache; or an ingenious eighteenth-century Italian painting whose strips turn to display the Three Ages of Man; all have a vinous association. It is wonderfully uncluttered and every piece of the highest quality in its genre. . . .

The *Musée du Vin* has steps leading down to another museum – the private and reserve cellars of wine. There is no wine in the Mouton cellar so old as that at Lafite and the oldest Mouton vintage in the private cellar is 1859, but there is a greater collection of old wines of its own and from other châteaux than any other, not excepting the fine collection at Château Margaux. There are 20,000–30,000 bottles in one cellar, 100,000 in another. The specially locked and segregated cellar of Mouton wines has a 'reference library' of twenty-four bottles, five magnums and two jeroboams of each vintage. In the older bins lie, like elephants half submerged in a sea of mud, ancient jeroboams and magnums encrusted with a dark kind of fungus which has almost to be chipped off when the bottle is taken out for its appointed day of opening. To the visitor the wealth of wine is inebriating without a bottle being opened. For example, I observed fifty-nine bottles, two magnums and two jeroboams of the famous 1870; but it would be difficult to call in vain for any vintage not lying there in considerable quantity. These bottles are re-corked and if necessary topped up from the same wine every twenty-five years; the last occasion was in 1957.

Edmund Penning-Rowsell, *The Wines of Bordeaux*, 1969

Red burgundy was saluted in one of the few modern poems on wine:

Praise now the ancient Duchy of the Vine
Where the warm tide of summer sunlight spills
On vineyards ranging along the Golden Hills,
Upbrimming every long and leafy line.

In grapes of Chambertin and Clos de Beze,
Richebourg, La Romanée, lie darkly curled
The purple kings of all the vinous world;
Till from the dusky fruit in autumn days

That juice is crushed which slowly, subtlely grows
Through hidden workings, whispered fomentations,
Like ghostly dancers mixed in strange mutations,
To essence of the ruby and the rose.

Be patient then, while generous years devise
Maturity and riches to the wine,
Till, to perfection come, it darkly shine
Upon the banquets of the truly wise.

Martin Armstrong, 'Burgundy', 1935

*And red burgundy – the greatest of red burgundies,
Romanée-Conti – is the subject of one of Cyril Ray's
characteristically warm, personal, amusing and memorable wine anecdotes.*

Better Moroccan red with one's best friend than
Mouton '53 at the hands of an editor who has asked
you to dinner to break it gently that he is giving you
the sack.

I think that over the years, fond as I am of the
light wines of Alsace and the Mosel, I have derived
more pleasure from red wines than from white. Indeed,
I have often felt a meal to be incomplete, even though
an exquisite white wine has accompanied a main
course of fish, if I have not finished with at any rate
a mouthful of even a very modest red with some cheese.
And, at least in recent years, claret has meant more
to me than burgundy.

This represents a change, or a development, of taste:
when I was young, I preferred burgundy. When I was
middle-aged, indeed. As recently as 1953, though I was
already a claret convert, I was still fighting something
of a rearguard action, and when I drove to Italy that
summer with my bride, I insisted on going by Route
Nationale 74, because we had introductions to one of

the great shippers of burgundy, and I wanted to show my wife, a dedicated claret-lover if ever there was one, that there was merit in a great burgundy, too: I had great hopes of a La Romanée-Conti 1934 that had been promised us by our friends.

We stood in their cellar, in a tiny tasting-room, and the cellarman glided in with the bottle in his hands, as though he were bearing a baby to the font. But the cellar was very deep; the tasting-room was very small; the smell of wine was strong; and my wife – tired from hours in an open car under the hot sun – had a sudden attack of claustrophobia. She dashed for the stairs just as the cellarman entered: I looked in agony from the bottle coming in to my bride going out – and I went out, too. Never let it be forgotten that, between bride and bottle, I chose bride. Just.

Cyril Ray, *In a Glass Lightly*, 1967

Returning to a textbook which is so much more than a textbook, we find this note on Montrachet:

Montrachet has a habit of being the one name people remember when they think of white burgundy. In the United States, where 'greatness' is at a premium, it is linked with Romanée-Conti, representing the best red burgundy, Château Lafite as the best claret and Château d'Yquem as the best white Bordeaux. Then comes Krug as the best champagne, Steinberger Kabinet or Schloss Vollrads as the best hock, Bernkasteler Doktor as the best Moselle. It is a simple and trouble-free approach to wine, and hideously expensive.

What is it that makes Montrachet stand out from the wines of the surrounding countryside, not as a giant among pigmies, but as a colossus among giants? It is simply the power and beauty of its taste. I will never forget a long tasting of new wines in the cellars of M. Remoissenet in Beaune, standing among the casks in the half-light... The wines were the new 1964s. We started by tasting four Meursaults – the peculiar mealy Meursault taste ran through them all.

Some brought it to more fruit, more freshness, more vitality than others. Les Perrières seemed to have most to offer.

Then followed the Montrachets; a clear ascent from a Puligny-Montrachet, a village wine (though a beauty, flowery and fresh), through Bâtard-Montrachet ('capped it completely; what could be more perfect?') to Le Montrachet. 'Still fermenting a little in its second fermentation,' I have down. 'Nevertheless a tremendous heady scent of peaches and apricots and an intense sweetness of character, though fully dry, in the mouth. It declares itself immediately to be something *very* special.'

That was Le Montrachet before it was even fully made, let alone bottled and ready to drink. What one can say is this: the character of Montrachet is that of the complete balanced white wine. It is sweet in its nature, yet there is no spare sugar; it is not syrupy, but dry and lively. It is soft to drink, but firm and clear-cut. It suggests, without imitating, all the ripest and most perfect of fruit.

Hugh Johnson, *Wine*, 1966

He follows it with a sensitive discussion of matching it with food.

It is difficult to know what to eat with a wine which has as much personality as Montrachet. I am of the school of thought which would drink it alone, if not, as Alexandre Dumas claimed was the correct procedure, kneeling, with head bared. I do not know the food that would not be completely overpowered by it.

I have enjoyed Le Montrachet immensely with a cold salmon-trout early in the summer, but that was not a wine of one of the great, powerful vintages, when ripeness makes it really full-blown in scent. I think I would fall back on a chicken, plainly roasted or grilled or even boiled. There is no better accompaniment to any great wine, white or red.

With Le Montrachet we are discussing the food that

goes with the wine; with its Montrachet cousins, for the most part, we are back in the realms where wine goes with food. Where do they fit in?

At dinners which aim to show the best of French (or indeed of any) wine against a formal menu, where fish comes before meat, white burgundy is almost always represented by a hyphenated Montrachet. The perfect menu, I have heard many good eaters say, has white burgundy for the first wine, claret for the second. White Bordeaux is never that wonderful. Red burgundy after white fails to use the amazing potential of France. Between them, white burgundy and claret represent the best of everything. In these circumstances there is no fish or shellfish which would not be a good match for a Meursault or a Puligny – or Chassagne-Montrachet. The same would be true of a meal in which fish was the main or the only dish. It is the quality of the fish, in fact, which is on trial in the presence of wines as delicious as these.

Hugh Johnson, *Wine*, 1966

On to the Rhône, and a charming picture of the country of Châteauneuf-du-Pape:

There was one, above all, a good old man named Boniface. Oh, as for him, what tears were shed in Avignon when he died! He was so amiable, so affable a prince! He laughed so heartily from the back of his mule! And when you passed near him, were you a poor little madderdyer or the grand provost of the town, he would give you his blessing so politely! A real Pope of Yvetot, but of a Provençal Yvetot, with a trace of shrewdness in his laugh, a sprig of marjoram in his biretta, and not a bit of Jeanneton. The only Jeanneton whom this good father was ever known to possess was his vineyard, – a little vineyard which he planted himself, three leagues from Avignon, among the myrtles of Château-Neuf.

Every Sunday, on coming from vespers, the worthy man would go and make love to it; and when he was up there, seated in the pleasant sunlight, with his mule near him and his cardinals all about him, lying at the foot of the trees, then he would have them uncork a flask of the wine of the vineyard, – that beautiful ruby-coloured wine which has since been called the Château-Neuf des Papes, – and would sip it, looking tenderly at his vineyard. Then, when the flask was empty and the night beginning to fall, he would return joyfully to the city, followed by his whole chapter; and when he passed over the bridge into Avignon, amidst the tambourines and the farandoles, his mule, excited by the music, would fall into a little skipping amble, while he himself would mark the measure of the dance with his biretta, – a thing which greatly scandalized his cardinals, but caused all the people to say: 'Ah, the kind prince! Ah, the good Pope!'

Alphonse Daudet, *Letters from my Mill*, 1866

The queen of sweet white wines of course is Château d'Yquem.

The universal place of pilgrimage in Sauternes is Château Yquem, whose labels, for some reason, call it Château d'Yquem. The château is one of the most impressive in all Bordeaux. It is what everyone hopes a château will be like, for it is one of the few which is a castle. The Middle Ages planted it soberly on its hilltop. The seventeenth century made it habitable – though by no means luxurious – and the twentieth century has perfected the symmetry of the rows of vines which march up the hill to it in an unbroken procession.

At Yquem every stage of wine-making is carried out with the loving care that goes into the manufacture of a Rolls-Royce. It is said to be the only place where all the wine-making machinery, without exception, is made of wood – even the intricate moving parts of presses – so that no metal ever comes in contact with the wine, in case it should affect its taste. They make what they firmly believe to be the best sweet drink in the world, and there are very few who would deny their claim. No trouble is too much for it. As a result even in poor years – though not in disastrous ones, when no wine is sold under the château's name – the wine they make is an astonishing mixture of richness and freshness. It is so rich as to feel almost like cream in your mouth, but strangely uncloying – its scent and flavour are so intense that they call you back to sniff and sip again.

The late Marquis de Lur Saluces, the proprietor of Yquem and one of the most distinguished figures of Bordeaux, held that his wine was good with several kinds of food. He drank it with *foie gras*. He once made me drink it with lobster. I am obviously not in a position to say that he was wrong. To me, though, it is still the wine to sip after – or indeed before – all others, quite by itself, not even with a peach or some grapes, as many people suggest. Its balance is perfect: why add the acidity which even a perfect peach cannot avoid? A wine like this is so much better than any mere fruit.

Hugh Johnson, *Wine*, 1966

Surely no wines of France are at once more uniformly high in quality or more sadly under-rated than those of Alsace – and they are versatile, too.

Dr Fritz Hallgarten has recorded a memorable Alsatian meal that was preceded by a young sylvaner, and then began with onion soup. Then pike and an older riesling, and a sip of the sylvaner, and then the main course – ham *en croûte* – with a pinot gris, or Alsatian tokay, and again a sip of the sylvaner, followed by cheeses from the Vosges accompanied by a gewürztraminer, followed by the sylvaner yet again before going on to sweetmeats, and back to the tokay that had been served with the ham. A meal notable for two things – not only for the use as a sort of sorbet between the courses of the wine that had been served as the aperitif, but where else in the world would you find a wine to go both with ham *en croûte* and with sweetmeats, as did that tokay d'Alsace?

Though I might have preferred, myself, with the pudding, the 1959 traminer *beerenauslese* that I drank with Jean Hugel and his wife in the gabled, half-timbered, whole-heartedly window-boxed and picture-postcarded Hansel-and-Gretel Alsatian town of Riquewihr, where the Hugels have been growers and shippers of wine since 1637. Only 753 bottles of the great dessert wine had been made, picked grape by grape as they withered into sultana-like sweetness on the vine – a wine with great sweetness and fruit, yet nothing like so lusciously sweet as a German wine of the same type, still less as sweet as a great Sauternes.

We drank it with an apricot-meringue confection of Madame's, and Jean Hugel swirled his glass and held it to his nose, looked reflectively into the middle distance for a moment, and then caught my eye, and gave the sort of shy, proud, half-smile that a father might give to a friend who watched with him as a son made a century at Lord's. Madame intercepted the glance, and turned to me with, 'Jean est amoureux de ses vins'. No wife could have been prouder of a husband's love-affairs.

Even now, well-known as they have become, the wines of Alsace do not come one's way as often as those of Germany, or as the French classics that are far older-established in the English market, such as claret, burgundy, or champagne. Which may be why I have never had a bad one – I have sometimes been disappointed in a sylvaner's lack of bouquet or, contrari-wise, by a traminer's tasting less bewitching than its scent had promised, but I have never known an Alsatian wine seem coarse, or ill-bred. Nor violent, either, though it may be that some day I shall be obliged to put to the test that renowned wine of Wolxheim, which they used to say would break a man's legs under him.

Cyril Ray, *In a Glass Lightly*, 1967

*Still among the white wines, this is a modern poet's
salute to German wine:*

Turn eastward, Bacchus: it is time to go
From Burgundy, Champagne, Cognac, Bordeaux,
Across the frontier. Here we shall replenish
Our empty cups with that pale amber Rhenish
Pressed from the clusters of your sacred vine
That clothes the hills of many-castled Rhine.
Choose well the route, for we must visit first
Rheinhessen, there to halt and quench our thirst
With Nierstein and the names of lesser breed
Whose limpid charm shall answer to our need
After the dusty march to Germany.
But when our wearied Mænads, putting by
The proffered cup, for richer draughts shall cry,
We'll turn aside their lickerish lust to sate
With odorous wines of the Palatinate
Whose short-lived beauty sickens and is dead
Ere nobler wines their callow youth have shed.
But we who tirelessly pursue the best
Must northward march to where the stream flows
    west

To Rheingau hills whose far-famed vineyards climb
From Hochheim on the Main to Rudesheim.
There in the shadow of some castled rock
We'll stretch at ease and sip the best of Hock,
Determining with learnèd tongue and nose
Whether the honeysuckle or the rose
Apes best these subtle essences that run
Through Nineteen-Twenty and Nineteen-Twenty-
    One.

Martin Armstrong, 'Hock', 1935

*Italian wines have a vast and even spectacular history;
but until lately little consistency of flavour. Now
heightened quality adds to their romantic aura. Once
again Cyril Ray captures atmosphere and character in
a few lines.*

In the very first weeks of the war, when I had been
sent to the London office before going off to the wars
for my paper, I would scour Soho to find a bottle of
rough Italian wine at a copper or so cheaper than the
one I had bought the other day, and teach myself by
adventurous trial and disastrous error why red wine
went better with meat than it did with fish; which
Italian wines were not only red but fizzy, and came
frothing out of the bottle like a mixture of Wincarnis
and Eno's; and why a sweet wine from Sicily, say,
tasting of muscatel grapes, was not the ideal accompaniment for the chop I had just charred on the minute
electric grill of my attic flat.

I do not think that I had then read a single book
about wine, and I could have saved myself many a
nasty taste in the mouth had I done so, but I was
giving myself a grounding, without particularly
noticing what I was doing, in some of the basic
principles of wine-drinking, and learning to understand
not only why one bottle of wine cost five or ten
times as much as another, but why it was worth it.

Before I came to such wines, though, there was one
more formative experience, and that was Italy. For a

time it was Apulia, the heel of Italy, where even in peacetime the wines are indifferent, and southern Italy at the time was cruelly deprived and devastated by war, even beyond its usual state of grinding poverty. But it was still a country where wine was a part of life – we picked the grapes from roadside vineyards to quench our thirst as the Eighth Army clanked and rumbled its way northwards in a cloud of dust – and where men grew wine as a matter of course, and put grimy carafes of it on the table at every meal, equally as a matter of course. And it is salutary for an Englishman to live for a while in a wine-growing country, even – or perhaps particularly – a wine-growing country as simple as Apulia, where wine is neither a symbol by which snobs can demonstrate their wealth or their taste, nor a means of fuddlement, but as natural and as necessary as bread.

The deep south of Italy is simple still. Only last year, touring Italy for a book I was writing on Italian wines, I came to Reggio di Calabria, in the toe, and was taken by an official of the wine-growers' association to a local cellar for a tasting. When I asked the cellarman what he called this that he was drawing from the cask, he said, '*vino*', and to my question, 'Yes, but what *vino*?' the answer was, '*vino rosso*'. He was neither joking nor sulking: he simply thought that I was momentarily at a loss for a common Italian word. Like many of his fellow wine-growers in the south, he would have been hard put to it to give a name to the grapes his wine was made from, and they came from no particular vineyard or commune, but simply from round about.

Cyril Ray, *In a Glass Lightly*, 1967

The Spanish wines, sherry apart, have only become popular in Britain in quite recent years but those prepared to taste in an open mind have long been aware of their quality.

If I were asked what I think is the best value for

money of any red wine in the world today – wine, that is, which is freely available – I would say Rioja, one of the old Reservas, wine fifteen or more years old, which is no harder to obtain than sherry, but which the majority of wine-merchants persist in ignoring.

The Rioja Reservas are like neither claret nor burgundy, nor any other French wine – and they do not claim to be. They have a style of their own; a very warm and smooth, velvety, very slightly roasted-tasting flavour. The lighter ones behave as a claret does after fifteen years or so – they begin to thin out a little, losing intensity and gaining delicacy. When the wine is good it grows fresher and sweeter with age.

The heavier ones stay stronger in flavour, but seem to radiate comfort and warmth like a roast chestnut. All have a subtle, fresh and somehow altogether Spanish smell.

While the best old Reservas have little to lose by being compared with fine French wines, the cheap ordinary red Rioja has everything to gain from being compared with its opposite number in France. It is in every way a better and more satisfying everyday drink than French *vin ordinaire*. The French wine has been blended so much that not even age will redeem it, while the natural, cheaply made but honest wine of Rioja gains enormously from a year or two in bottle.

Hugh Johnson, *Wine*, 1966

The table-wines of Portugal, too, have often been underestimated. Consider, for instance, Colares.

Colares has the greatest reputation among Portuguese red wines. It is grown under unusual conditions, which gives it the distinction of being one of the very few vineyards of Europe which has never had the plague of phylloxera, and does not need to graft its vine-stock on to American roots. The vines are planted in deep sand; the only kind of earth inimical to the destructive beetle.

Real Colares wine is made of one grape, the Ramisco,

a small, blue, dusty looking grape which gives it great colour. Recently, farmers have been planting others which are easier to grow and make softer wine which can be drunk younger, but the new kind of Colares has no real distinction, none of the character which made its name. The grand old Palacio Seteais hotel at Sintra still had the 1931 Colares of Tavares & Rodrigues in 1970; it was a beautiful wine, like a strong, soft claret, still very dark in colour despite its age. Such wine is still being made, and still needs a good deal of maturing – though not necessarily for thirty-nine years – but it is not what you are given if you ask for Colares without qualification.

Hugh Johnson, *Wine*, 1966

Port, of course, has entered into the British attitude to civilization.

'Cellars are not catacombs. They are, if rightly constructed, rightly considered, cloisters, where the bottle meditates on joys to bestow, not on dust misused! Have you anything great?'

'A great wine aged ninety.'

'Is it associated with your pedigree, that you pronounce the age with such assurance?'

'My grandfather inherited it.'

'Your grandfather, Sir Willoughby, had meritorious offspring, not to speak of generous progenitors. What would have happened had it fallen into the female line! I shall be glad to accompany you. Port? Hermitage?'

'Port.'

'Ah! we are in England!'

'There will just be time,' said Sir Willoughby, inducing Dr Middleton to step out.

A chirrup was in the Rev. Doctor's tone: 'Hocks, too, have compassed age. I have tasted senior Hocks. Their flavours are as a brook of many voices: they have depth also. Senatorial Port! we say. We cannot say that of any other wine. Port is deep-sea deep. It is in its flavour deep – mark the difference. It is like a classic tragedy, organic in conception. An ancient Hermitage has the light of the antique; the merit that it can grow to an extreme old age; a merit. Neither of Hermitage nor of Hock can you say that it is the blood of those long years, retaining the strength of youth with the wisdom of age. To Port for that! Port is our noblest legacy! Observe, I do not compare the wines; I distinguish the qualities. Let them live together for enrichment; they are not rivals like the Idaean Three. Were they rivals, a fourth would challenge them. Burgundy has great genius. It does wonders within its period; it does all except to keep up in the race; it is shortlived. An aged Burgundy runs with a beardless Port. I cherish the fancy that Port speaks the sentences of wisdom, Burgundy sings in inspired Ode. Or put it, that Port is the Homeric hexameter, Burgundy the Pindaric dithyramb. What do you say?'

George Meredith, *The Egoist*, 1879

It was memorably the wine of one of the great Englishmen of fiction:

The wine circulated languidly, and Mr Jorrocks in vain tried to get up a conversation on hunting. The Professor always started his stones or Mr Muleygrubs his law, varied by an occasional snore from Mr Slowman, who had to be nudged by Jones every time the bottle went round. Thus they battled on for about an hour.

'Would *you* like any more wine?' at length inquired Mr Muleygrubs, with a motion of rising.

'Not any more I'm obleged to you,' replied the obsequious Mr Jacob Jones, who was angling for the chaplaincy of Mr Marmaduke's approaching shrievalty.

'Just another bottle!' rejoined Mr Jorrocks encouragingly.

'Take a glass of claret,' replied Mr Muleygrubs, handing the jug to our master.

'Rayther not, thank ye,' replied Mr Jorrocks, 'not

the stuff for me. By the way now, I should think,'
continued Mr Jorrocks, with an air of sudden en-
lightenment, 'that some of those old ancient ancestors
o' yours have been fond o' claret.'

'Why so?' replied Mr Muleygrubs pertly.

'Doesn't know,' replied Mr Jorrocks, musingly, 'but
I never hears your name mentioned without thinking
o' small claret. But come, let's have another bottle o'
black strap – it's good strap – sound and strong – got
wot I calls a good grib o' the gob.'

'Well,' said Mr Muleygrubs, getting up and ringing
the bell, 'if you must, you must, but I should think
you have had enough.'

'PORT WINE!' exclaimed he, with the air of a man
with a dozen set out, to his figure footman, as he
answered the bell.

R. S. Surtees, *Handley Cross*, 1843

*North America has long produced wines of varying
merit. In the last two or three decades, though, it has
become increasingly well produced, fashionable and
popular; especially that produced in California. In the
last century one of the most popular – esteemed in
Britain as well as America – was Catawba, from Ohio,
then the most important United States' production
area. It was saluted by one of the country's major poets.*

This song of mine
Is a Song of the Vine
To be sung by the glowing embers
Of wayside inns,
When the rain begins
To darken the drear Novembers.

It is not a song
Of the Scuppernong,
From warm Carolinian valleys,
Nor the Isabel
And the Muscadel
That bask in our garden alleys.

[70]

Nor the red Mustang,
Whose clusters hang
O'er the waves of the Colorado,
And the fiery flood
Of whose purple blood
Has a dash of Spanish bravado.

For richest and best
Is the wine of the West,
That grows by the Beautiful River;
Whose sweet perfume
Fills all the room
With a benison on the giver.

And as hollow trees
Are the haunts of bees,
For ever going and coming;
So this crystal hive
Is all alive
With a swarming and buzzing and humming.

Very good in its way
Is the Verzenay,
Or the Sillery soft and creamy;
But Catawba wine
Has a taste more divine,
More dulcet, delicious, and dreamy.

There grows no vine
By the haunted Rhine,
By Danube or Guadalquivir,
Nor on island or cape,
That bears such a grape
As grows by the Beautiful River.

Drugged is their juice
For foreign use,
When shipped o'er the reeling Atlantic,
To rack our brains
With the fever pains,
That have driven the Old World frantic.

To the sewers and sinks
With all such drinks,
And after them tumble the mixer:
For a poison malign
Is such Borgia wine,
Or at best but a Devil's Elixir.

While pure as a spring
Is the wine I sing,
And to praise it, one needs but to name it:
For Catawba wine
Has need of no sign,
No tavern-bush to proclaim it.

And this Song of the Vine,
This greeting of mine,
The winds and the birds shall deliver
To the Queen of the West,
In her garlands dressed,
On the banks of the Beautiful River.

Henry Wadsworth Longfellow (1807–82),
'Catawba Wine'

Unwise, Over-Wined

Three of the sharpest definitions in the sharpest of all dictionaries concern drinking.

ALCOHOL, *n.* (Arabic *al kohl*, a paint for the eyes.) The essential principle of all such liquids as give a man a black eye.

DRUNK, *adj.* Boozy, fuddled, corned, tipsy, mellow, soaken, full, groggy, tired, top-heavy, glorious, overcome, swipy, elevated, overtaken, screwed, raddled, lushy, nappy, muzzy, maudlin, pious, floppy, loppy, happy, etc.

WINE, *n.* Fermented grape juice known to the Womens' Christian Union as 'liquor', sometimes as 'rum'. Wine, madam, is God's next best gift to man.

Ambrose Bierce, *The Devil's Dictionary*, 1906

For the wise, drunkenness is the worst end of drinking. The drunkard was most effectively and salutarily described over three and a half centuries ago.

A Drunkard is a noun-adjective; for he cannot stand alone by himself; yet in his greatest weakness a great tryer of strength, whether health or sickness will have the upper hand in a surfeit. He is a spectacle of deformity and a shame of humanity, a view of sin, and a grief of nature. He is the annoyance of modesty and the trouble of civility, the spoil of wealth and the spite of reason. He is only the brewer's agent and the ale-house's benefactor, the beggar's companion and the constable's trouble. He is his wife's woe, his children's sorrow, his neighbours' scoff and his own shame. In sum, he is a tub of swill, a spirit of sleep, a picture of a beast and a monster of a man.

Nicholas Breton, *The Good and the Bad*, 1616

Even the pious George Herbert was scathing on the subject –

> He that is drunken, may his mother kill
> Big with his sister; he hath lost the reins,
> Is outlawed by himself: all kinds of ill
> Did with his liquor slide into his veins

George Herbert, 'The Temple', 1633

The Bible is cautionary:

Who hath woe? Who hath sorrow? Who hath contentions? Who hath babbling? Who hath wounds without cause? Who hath redness of eyes?

They that tarry long at the wine; they that go to seek mixed wine.

Look not thou upon the wine when it is red, when it giveth his colour in the cup, when it moveth itself aright.

At the last it biteth like a serpent, and stingeth like an adder.

Proverbs 23: 29–32

Dr Johnson was both more trenchant and more acid:

On Wednesday, April 7th, I dined with him at Sir Joshua Reynolds's.

I have not marked what company was there. Johnson harangued upon the qualities of different liquors; and spoke with great contempt of claret, as so weak, that 'a man would be drowned by it before it made him drunk.' He was persuaded to drink one glass of it, that he might judge, not from recollection, which might be dim, but from immediate sensation. He shook his head, and said, 'Poor stuff. No, Sir, claret is the liquor for boys; port for men: but he who aspires to be a hero (smiling) must drink brandy. In the first place, the flavour of brandy is most grateful to the palate; and then brandy will do soonest for a man what drinking can do for him. There are indeed, few who are able to drink brandy. This is a power rather to be wished for than attained. And yet (proceeded he) as in all pleasure hope is a considerable part, I know not but the fruition comes too quickly by brandy. Florence wine I think the worst; it is wine only to the eye; it is wine neither while you are drinking it, nor after you have drunk it; it neither pleases the taste, nor exhilarates the spirits.' I reminded him how heartily he and I used to drink wine together when we were first acquainted; and how I used to have a headache after sitting up with him. He did not like to have this recalled, or, perhaps, thinking that I boasted improperly, resolved to have a witty stroke at me: 'Nay, Sir, it was not the wine that made your head ache, but the sense that I put into it.' BOSWELL: 'What Sir! will sense make the head ache?' JOHNSON: 'Yes, Sir, (with a smile) when it is not used to it.' No man who has a true relish of pleasantry could be offended at this; especially if Johnson in a long intimacy had given him repeated proofs of his regard and good estimation. I used to say, that as he had given me a thousand pounds in praise, he had a good right now and then to take a guinea from me.

James Boswell, *Life of Johnson*, 1791

If all drunkards are to be pitied, the anonymous drunkard is at most a generalization. The famous drunks – especially those of the Georgian and Regency periods – are followed through all history by the gossips.

The Duke of Norfolk, called Jockey of Norfolk in his time, was celebrated for his table exploits. He had quarrelled with the Regent, like the rest of the Whigs; but a sort of reconciliation had taken place; and now, being a very old man, the prince invited him to dine and sleep at the Pavilion; and the old duke drove over from his Castle of Arundel with his famous equipage of grey horses, still remembered in Sussex.

The Prince of Wales had concocted with his royal

brothers a notable scheme for making the old man drunk. Every person at table was enjoined to drink wine with the duke – a challenge which the old toper did not refuse. He soon began to see that there was a conspiracy against him; he drank glass for glass; he overthrew many of the brave. At last the First Gentleman of Europe proposed bumpers of brandy. One of the royal brothers filled a great glass for the duke. He stood up and tossed off the drink. 'Now,' says he, 'I will have my carriage, and go home.' The prince urged upon him his previous promise to sleep under the roof where he had been so generously entertained. 'No,' he said, he had had enough of such hospitality. A trap had been set for him; he would leave the place at once and never enter its doors more.

T. G. Shaw, *Wine, The Vine, and the Cellar*, 1863

This piece of gossip stems from the same family; about the Duke of York, the brother with whom George IV had many a midnight carouse, of whom –

'I remember,' says Pückler, 'that one evening – indeed, it was past midnight – he took some of his guests, among whom were the Austrian ambassador, Count Meervelt, Count Beroldingen, and myself, into his beautiful armoury. We tried to swing several Turkish sabres, but none of us had a very firm grasp; whence it happened that the duke and Meervelt both scratched themselves with a sort of straight Indian sword, so as to draw blood. Meervelt then wished to try if the sword cut as well as a Damascus, and attempted to cut through one of the wax candles that stood on the table. The experiment answered so ill, that both the candles, candlesticks and all, fell to the ground and were extinguished. While we were groping in the dark and trying to find the door, the duke's aide-de-camp stammered out in great agitation, "By G—, sir, I remember the sword is poisoned!"

'You may conceive the agreeable feelings of the wounded at this intelligence! Happily, on further examination, it appeared that claret, and not poison, was at the bottom of the colonel's exclamation.'

T. G. Shaw, *Wine, The Vine, and the Cellar*, 1863

George IV, the 'First Gentleman of Europe' was responsible for the appalling extravagance called 'Regent's Punch':

Three bottles of Champagne, two of Madeira, one of Hock, one of Curaçao, one quart of Brandy, one pint of Rum and two bottles of seltzer-water, flavoured with four pounds of bloom raisins, Seville oranges, lemons, white sugar-candy, and diluted with iced green tea instead of water.

As of the monarchs, so, often, of their statesmen:

As showing the training in sobriety that many of our leading statesmen at this time received it is told of Walpole that when he was quite a young man his father was accustomed to give him a double quantity of wine to that which he took for himself, saying, 'Come, Robert, you shall drink twice while I drink once, for I will not permit my son in his sober senses to be witness of the intoxication of his father.'

So it was said of Pitt the Younger:

During his boyhood, Pitt was very weakly; and his physician, Addington (Lord Sidmouth's father) ordered him to take port wine in large quantities: the consequence was, that, when he grew up, he could not do without it. Lord Grenville has seen him swallow a bottle of port in tumblerfuls, before going to the House. This, together with his habit of eating late suppers (indigestible cold veal-pies, etc.), helped undoubtedly to shorten his life. Huskisson, speaking to me of Pitt, said that his hands shook so much, that, when he helped himself to salt, he was obliged to support the right hand with the left.

Stothard the painter happened to be one evening at

an inn on the Kent Road, when Pitt and Dundas put up there on their way from Walmer. Next morning, as they were stepping into their carriage, the waiter said to Stothard, 'Sir, do you observe these two gentlemen?' – 'Yes,' he replied; 'and I know them to be Mr Pitt and Mr Dundas'. – 'Well, sir, how much wine do you suppose they drank last night?' – Stothard could not guess. – 'Seven bottles, sir'.

Samuel Rogers, Table Talk, 1856

Of the same pair of boon companions, Henry Dundas, 1st Viscount Melville (the friend of Shelburne, and the guide of Pitt) and the Younger Pitt, a conversation is reported:

PITT: 'I can't see the Speaker, Hal, can you?'
DUNDAS: 'Not see the Speaker, Billy? I see two.'

An earlier major figure, Steele of The Tatler, used in his cups to feel the deepest affection (even in her absence) for that Mrs Scurlock whom he met at the funeral of his first wife, and eventually married.

Saturday Night [August 30, 1707]

Dear, lovely Mrs *Scurlock,*

I have been in very good company, where your unknown name, under the character of the woman I lov'd best, has been often drunk; so that I may say I am dead drunk for your sake, which is more than I *dye for you.*

Eleven at Night [Jan. 5, 1708]

Dear *Prue,*

I was going home two hours ago, but was met by Mr *Griffith,* who has kept me ever since meeting me as he came from Mr *Lambert's.* I will come within a pint of wine.

We drink yr health, and Mr *Griffith* is yr ser'nt.

[Oct. 25, 1708]

Dear *Prue*,

If you do not hear of me before three to-morrow afternoon, believe I am too fuddled to take care to observe yr orders; but, however, know me to be yr most faithful, affectionate husband and ser'nt.

[Nov. 18, 1712]

Dear *Prue*,

I am come from a committee where I have [been] chairman, and drank too much. I have the headach, and should be glad you would come to me in good-humour, which would always banish any uneasiness of temper from, dear *Prue*, yr fond fool of a husband.

[Feb. 16, 1716–17]

Dear *Prue*,

Sober or not, I am ever yours.

Sir Richard Steele, *Letters*

Steele at other times proved himself a quite brilliant journalist on the subject of wine:

There is in this city a certain fraternity of chemical operators who work underground in holes, coverns, and dark retirements, to conceal their mysteries from the eyes and observations of mankind. These subterraneous philosophers are daily employed in the transmutation of liquors, and, by the power of magical drugs and incantations, raising under the streets of London the choicest products of the hills and valleys of France. They can squeeze Bordeaux out of the sloe, and draw champagne from an apple. Virgil, in that remarkable prophecy,

Incultisque rubens pendebit sentibus uva,
The rip'ning grape shall hang on every thorn,

seems to have hinted at this art, which can turn a plantation of northern hedges into a vineyard. These adepts are known among one another by the name of 'winebrewers', and, I am afraid, do great injury, not only to Her Majesty's customs, but to the bodies of many of her good subjects.

Having received sundry complaints against these invisible workmen, I ordered the proper officer of my court to ferret them out of their respective caves, and bring them before me, which was yesterday executed accordingly.

The person who appeared against them was a merchant who had by him a great magazine of wines that he had laid in before the war; but these gentlemen, as he said, had so vitiated the nation's palate, that no man could believe his to be French, because it did not taste like what they sold for such. He then enlarged, with a great show of reason, upon the prejudice which these mixtures and compositions had done to the brains of the English nation; as is too visible, said he, from many late pamphlets, speeches, and sermons, as well as from the ordinary conversations of the youth of this age. In particular, he asserted most of the modern enthusiasms and agitations to be nothing else but the effects of adulterated Port.

The counsel for the brewers had a face so extremely inflamed and illuminated with carbuncles, that I did not wonder to see him an advocate for these sophistications. Indeed, I was so surprised at his figure and parts, that I ordered him to give me a taste of his usual liquor; which I had no sooner drunk, but I found a pimple rising in my forehead; and felt such a sensible decay in my understanding that I would not proceed in the trial until the fume of it was entirely dissipated.

Sir Richard Steele, *The Tatler*, c. 1709–11

David Copperfield, who began with beer, became the most human of all Dickens's wine drinkers. Indeed, it is difficult to escape the conclusion that there was something autobiographical in David's first bachelor party, at Mrs Crupp's lodging:

Everything was very good; we did not spare the wine.
I went on, by passing the wine faster and faster yet,
and continually starting up with a cockscrew to open
more wine, long before any was needed. I proposed
Steerforth's health. I said he was my dearest friend,
the protector of my boyhood, and the companion of
my prime. I said I was delighted to propose his health.
I said I owed him more obligations than I could ever
repay, and held him in a higher admiration than I
could ever express. I finished by saying, 'I'll give you
Steerforth! God bless him! Hurrah!' We gave him three
times three, and another, and a good one to finish
with. I broke my glass in going round the table to
shake hands with him, and I said (in two words)
'Steerforth, you'retheguidingstarofmyexistence...'

Somebody was leaning out of my bedroom window,
refreshing his forehead against the cool stone of the
parapet, and feeling the air upon his face. It was
myself. I was addressing myself as 'Copperfield', and
saying 'Why did you try to smoke? You might have
known you couldn't do it.'

Steerforth said, 'You are all right, Copperfield, are
you not?' and I told him, 'Neverberrer'...

Charles Dickens, *David Copperfield*, 1849–50

*The professions have thrown up an impressive soak
of topers:*

At Edinburgh, the old judges had a practice at which
even their age used to shake its head. They had always
wine and biscuits *on the Bench*, when the business
was clearly to be protracted beyond the usual dinner
hour. The modern judges – those I mean who were
made after 1800, never gave in to this; but with those
of the preceding generation, some of whom lasted
several years after 1800, it was quite common. Black
bottles of strong port were set down beside them on
the Bench, with glasses, caraffes of water, tumblers,
and biscuits; and this without the slightest attempt at

concealment. The refreshment was generally allowed
to stand untouched for a short time, as if despised,
during which their Lordships seemed to be intent only
on their notes. But in a little, some water was poured
into the tumbler, and sipped quietly as if merely to
sustain nature. Then a few drops of wine were ventured
upon, but only with the water. But at last patience
could endure no longer, and a full bumper of the pure
black element was tossed over; after which the thing
went on regularly, and there was a comfortable munch-
ing and quaffing to the great envy of the parched
throats in the gallery. The strong-headed stood it toler-
ably well, but it told, plainly enough, upon the feeble.
Not that the ermine was absolutely intoxicated, but it
was certainly sometimes affected. This however was so
ordinary with these sages, that it really made little
apparent change upon them. It was not very perceptible
at a distance; and they all acquired the habit of sitting
and looking judicial enough, even when their bottles
had reached the lowest ebb.

This open-court refection did not prevail, so far as
I ever saw, at Circuits. It took a different form there.
The temptation of the inn frequently produced a total
stoppage of business; during which all concerned –
judges and counsel, clerks, jurymen, and provost, had
a jolly dinner; after which they returned to the
transportations and hangings. I have seen this done
often. It was a common remark that the step of the
evening procession was far less true to the music than
that of the morning.

Henry, Lord Cockburn, *Memorials*, 1856

Still within the law –

When I was a child, I saw the famous Sir Toby Butler,
a favourite lawyer of his time, his powers of oratory
being great; but he always drank his bottle before he
went to the courts. A client, very solicitous about the
success of his cause, requested Sir Toby not to drink

his accustomed bottle that morning. Sir Toby promised on his honour he would not. He went to the court, pleaded, and gained a verdict. The client met him exulting in the success of his advice; when, to his astonishment, Sir Toby assured him that if he had *not* taken his bottle, he should have lost the cause. 'But your promise, Sir Toby?' – 'I kept it faithfully and honourably, I did not *drink* a drop – I poured my bottle of claret into a wheaten loaf and *ate* it. So I had my bottle, you your verdict, and I am a man of my word.'

John O'Keeffe, *Recollections*, 1826

Another heavy drinking story comes from the medical profession:

Doctor Fordyce sometimes drank a good deal at dinner. He was summoned one evening to see a lady patient, when he was more than half-seas-over, and conscious that he was so. Feeling her pulse, and finding himself unable to count its beats, he muttered, 'Drunk, by God!' Next morning, recollecting the circumstance, he was greatly vexed: and just as he was thinking what explanation of his behaviour he should offer to the lady, a letter from her was put into his hand. 'She too well knew', said the letter, 'that he had discovered the unfortunate condition in which she was when he last visited her; and she entreated him to keep the matter secret in consideration of the enclosed (a hundred-pound bank-note).'

Samuel Rogers, *Table Talk*, 1856

A shrewd observer of drinking habits, including his own, was John Bernard.

Sir John Danvers lived well, as the gout in his left leg testified. He usually took his three bottles, which he called his three friends: the first, his encourager; the second, his adviser; and the third, his consoler. He had also a humorous knack of bestowing upon wine a regal appellation, and making its various species represent, when placed upon the table, the sovereigns of the countries that produced them: – thus, a bottle of port stood for the King of Portugal, champagne for that of France, Madeira for his Spanish Majesty, whilst a bottle of porter, I believe, represented our beloved Monarch. If we turned, therefore, from one wine to another, he would exclaim, 'Now we have bled the King of Spain to death, what if we decapitate the King of France!'

John Bernard, *Retrospections of the Stage*, 1830

The same student extended his observation to Ireland:

I was led to observe, for the first time, the hard-drinking which prevailed in the interior. At the table of Mr Rice, Sir John O'Neil, and the Belfast society in general, it was the custom to put a bottle of wine at each person's elbow, and let him fill as he pleased; but here were particular meetings, where bumpers were drunk for the evening out of half-pint goblets, – which were without a stand, in order to compel the bibber to empty their contents at a draught. This race of convivialists (who, from their strong heads and capacious entrails, were denominated by their brother Bacchanals – the 'six-bottle men') were chiefly composed of old fox-hunters and country 'squires; and, like certain plants, seemed only to be kept alive by perpetual soaking. But these persons were not to be stigmatized as drunkards: their drink was claret, a light wine (wanting its modern spirit, brandy); habit had rendered this extraordinary means of vivification harmless. Those who suffered from their system were strangers who had not been schooled in it (and in this way the old saying of 'killing with kindness' was very literally verified); but it was a surprising event indeed if one of the 'initiated' could not, after making a cellarage of his stomach, and stowing away his half-dozen, maintain the perpendicularity of his attitude with the most mathematical precision.

John Bernard, *Retrospections of the Stage*, 1830

To progress from the merely heavy drinkers to the prodigious, we may take awed note of a legendary figure of Georgian times:

It is written of Hercules, that he acquired his immense strength by feeding on the marrow of lions; and how powerful must have been the stimulus of the almost unheard-of quantity of from *four to six* bottles of port wine *daily*, on that volcanic excitability of mind which was, not only by nature, Mr Mytton's, but which had been acted upon, and increased, by a severe affection of the brain at an early period of life! Thus, then, although I offer no excuse for his drinking, his drinking – for men are tried by wine, says the proverb, as metals are by fire – furnishes excuses, I should rather have said apologies, for his conduct, inasmuch as his reason was, to a certain extent, lost in delirium, caused by the fumes of wine on an already somewhat distempered brain. Many of his acts were not the acts of John Mytton, but of a man *mad, half by nature, and half by wine;* and I think his best and dearest friends are decidedly of my opinion.

From this account of its host, it may be supposed that Halston was a scene of general dissipation and riot. By no means. In short, I cannot bring to my recollection a single instance of being one of what may be termed a drunken party during my frequent visits to the house. But this is accounted for in more ways than one. The host had always the start of his friends, in the first place; and in the next, long sittings were not in accordance with his restless disposition. In the summer, he would jump out of the window, and be off. In the winter, he was anxious to get to the billiard-table, which was always lighted up after coffee, for the amusement of himself and his friends; and here he was in his element. How then, it may be asked, did he consume that quantity of port wine? Why this question is easily answered. He shaved with a bottle of it on his toilet; he worked steadily at it throughout the day, by a glass or two at a time, and at least a bottle with his luncheon; and the after-dinner and *after-supper* work – not losing sight of it in the billiard-room – completed the Herculean task ... He is, however, a memorable example of the comparatively harmless effects of *very good wine*, which he always had, and just of a proper age – about eight years old – for, assisted by exercise, such as he took, it was many years before it injured him. But, alas! wine at length lost its charms; brandy – which he was a stranger to when I was last at Halston – was substituted, and the constitution of John Mytton, *perhaps the hardest ever bestowed upon man*, was not proof against that.

'Nimrod' (C. J. Apperley), *The Life of John Mytton*,
1837

Among the mighty swiggers was Peter the Great of Russia, also the author of such mock-religious parodies as this:

> In the name of all drunkards,
> In the name of all tipplers,
> In the name of all fools,
> In the name of all clowns,
> In the name of all want-wits,
> In the name of all vodkas,
> In the name of all wines,
> In the name of all beers,
> In the name of all flasks,
> In the name of all pots,

In the name of all barrels,
In the name of all buckets,
In the name of all mugs,
In the name of all glasses and cups,
In the name of all cards, dice, and spillikins,
In the name of all tobaccos and taverns,
For there is the dwelling of our father, *Bacchus*.

Amen.

Peter the Great (1672–1725), 'Bacchus'

It is, too, credibly reported of him, and his company in Britain, that they were trenchermen of superhuman capacity.

The capacity of the Russians for food and drink always made a sensation. On a journey to Portsmouth, Peter and his party stayed at Godalming, where they sat down thirteen for supper and consumed five ribs of beef weighing three stone, a sheep, three-quarters of a lamb, a shoulder and a loin of veal, eight pullets and eight rabbits, and drank two and a half dozen bottles of sack, a dozen bottles of burgundy and unlimited beer, and had six quarts of mulled sack before going to bed. Before starting off the next morning they breakfasted on three quarts of brandy, half a sheep, nineteen pounds of lamb, seven dozen eggs, ten pullets and a dozen chickens.

Christopher Marsden, *Palmyra of the North*

[87]

The greatest swallower of them all, however, if he himself is to be believed, was a sixteenth-century man of the church who kept his own score.

Brethren, it is written, 'wine maketh glad the heart of man'... Now there is, doubtless, none of my male hearers who cannot drink his four bottles without affecting his brain. Let him, however – if by the fifth or sixth bottle he no longer knoweth his own wife – if he beat and kick his children, and look upon his dearest friend as an enemy – refrain ... But whosoever, after drinking his ten or twelve bottles, retains his senses sufficiently to support his tottering neighbour ... let him take his share quietly, and be thankful for his talent ... It is but seldom that our kind Creator extends to anyone the grace to be able to drink safely sixteen bottles, of which privilege he hath held me, the meanest of his servants, worthy.

Bishop of Treves

The closing note of this section must be that of the remorseful aftermath which demanded a great writer to describe it – and found him in Scotland.

Madam,

I dare say that this is the first epistle you ever received from this nether world. I write you from the regions of Hell, amid the horrors of the damn'd. The time and manner of my leaving your earth I do not exactly know, as I took my departure in the heat of a fever of intoxication, contracted at your too hospitable mansion; but, on my arrival here, I was fairly tried, and sentenced to endure the purgatorial tortures of this infernal confine for the space of ninety-nine years, eleven months and, twenty-nine days, and all on account of the impropriety of my conduct yesternight under your roof. Here am I, laid on a bed of pitiless furze, with my aching head reclined on a pillow of ever-piercing thorn, while an infernal tormentor, wrinkled, and old, and cruel, his name I think is *Recollection*, with a whip of scorpions, forbids peace or rest to approach me, and keeps anguish eternally awake. Still, Madam, if I could in any measure be reinstated in the good opinion of the fair circle whom my conduct last night so much injured, I think it would be an alleviation to my torments. For this reason I trouble you with this letter. To the men of the company I will make no apology. – Your husband, who insisted on my drinking more than I chose, has no right to blame me; and the other gentlemen were partakers of my guilt. But to you, Madam, I have much to apologize. Your good opinion I valued as one of the greatest acquisitions I had made on earth, and I was truly a beast to forfeit it. There was a Miss I— too, a woman of fine sense, gentle and unassuming manners – do make, on my part, a miserable damn'd wretch's best apology to her. A Mrs G—, a charming woman, did me the honour to be prejudiced in my favour; this makes me hope that I have not outraged her beyond all forgiveness. – To all the other ladies please present my humblest contrition for my conduct, and my petition for their gracious pardon. O all ye powers of decency and decorum! whisper to them that my errors, though great, were involuntary – that an intoxicated man is the vilest of beasts – that it was not in my nature to be brutal to any one – that to be rude to a woman, when in my senses, was impossible with me – but –

. . .

Regret! Remorse! Shame! ye three hellhounds that ever dog my steps and bay at my heels, spare me! spare me!

Forgive the offences, and pity the perdition of, Madam,

Your humble Slave,

(Robt. Burns)

Letter to Mrs Robert Riddell, 1793 (?)

Laughter in the Glass

The humour of drinking, as might be expected, is generally earthy, though sometimes touched with wit.

The English have a miraculous power of turning wine into water.

Oscar Wilde (1854–1900)

In the same strain, though earlier, is this comment:

Some men are like musical glasses – to produce their finest tones you must keep them wet.

Samuel Taylor Coleridge, *Table Talk*, 1835

A slightly more charitable, though class-conscious attitude lies in

> The rich man has a cellar,
> And a ready butler by him;
> The poor must steer
> For his pint of beer
> Where the saint can't choose but spy him.
>
> Thomas Love Peacock (1785–1866), 'The
> Poor Man's Lot'

There is an arrogant aloofness in this Scottish comment:

Wine is the drink of the gods, milk the drink of babies, tea the drink of women, and water the drink of beasts.

John Stuart Blackie (*fl.* 1860)

and a hearty earthiness in the jingle

> Here's to mine and here's to thine!
> Now's the time to clink it!
> Here's a flagon of old wine,
> And here we are to drink it!
>
> Nineteenth-century toast

In his last binn Sir Peter lies,
    Who knew not what it was to frown:
Death took him mellow, by surprise,
    And in his cellar stopped him down.
Through all our land we could not boast
    A knight more gay, more prompt than he,
To rise and fill a bumper toast,
    And pass it round with THREE TIMES THREE.

None better knew the feast to sway,
    Or keep Mirth's boat in better trim:
For Nature had but little clay
    Like that of which she moulded him.
The meanest guest that graced his board
    Was there the freest of the free,
His bumper toast when Peter poured,
    And passed it round with THREE TIMES THREE.

He kept at true good humour's mark,
    The social flow of pleasure's tide:
He never made a brow look dark,
    Nor caused a tear, but when he died.
No sorrow round his tomb should dwell:
    More pleased his gay old ghost would be,
For funeral song, and passing bell,
    To hear no sound but THREE TIMES THREE.

                    Thomas Love Peacock, 'Headlong Hall', 1816

I've heard him renounce wine a hundred times a day,
but then it has been between as many glasses.

                    Douglas Jerrold, c. 1840

I drink when I have occasion, and sometimes when I
have no occasion.

                    Miguel Cervantes, Don Quixote, 1605, 1615

    For the want of a drop of good beer,
    Drives lots to tipple more dear;

And they licks their wives
And destroys their lives,
Which they wouldn't have done upon beer!

Anon., nineteenth-century music-hall jingle

If with water you fill up your glasses,
You'll never write anything wise
But wine is the horse of Parnassus,
That carries a bard to the skies.

Athenaeus, *Deipnosophistai, c.* AD 200

The man that isn't jolly after drinking
Is just a drivelling idiot, to my thinking.

Euripides (according to Rabelais)

*To end this section on a note not merely of humour
but of good humour:*

I gave her cakes; I gave her ale,
I gave her sack and sherry;
I kist her once, I kist her twice,
And we were wondrous merry.

I gave her beads and bracelets fine,
And I gave her gold down derry,
I thought she was afear'd till she stroked my
beard,
And we were wondrous merry.

Merry my heart, merry my cocks, merry my
sprights,
Merry my hey down derry,
I kist her once and I kist her twice,
And we were wondrous merry.

Henry Purcell (1658?–95), *The Catch Club Collection*

The Laureate of Wine

A *number of writers have contributed measurably to the literature of wine but perhaps no one so frequently or in such varying vein as Byron. In almost all his writing the subject seems to occur appositely*:

Sweet is old wine in bottles, ale in barrels...

Few things surpass old wine; and they may preach
  Who please – the more because they preach in
  vain, –
Let us have wine and women, mirth and laughter,
Sermons and soda-water the day after.

. . .

Wine cheers the sad, revives the old, inspires
The young, makes weariness forget his toil,
  And fear her danger; opens a new world
When this, the present, falls.

Don Juan, Cantos I, II, 1819–24

I am but just returned to town, from which you may infer that I have been out of it; and I have been boxing, for exercise, with Jackson for this last month daily. I have also been drinking, and, on one occasion, with three other friends at the Cocoa Tree, from six till four, yea, unto five in the matin. We clareted and champagned till two – then supped, and finished with a kind of regency punch composed of madeira, brandy, and *green* tea, no *real* water being admitted therein. That was a night for you! without once quitting the table, except to ambulate home, which I did alone, and in utter contempt of a hackney-coach and my own *vis*, both of which were deemed necessary for our conveyance. And so, – I am very well, and they say it will hurt my constitution.

Letter to Thomas Moore, 9 April 1814

Yesterday, I dined out with a large-ish party, where were Sheridan and Colman, Harry Harris of C.G., and his brother, Sir Gilbert Heathcote, Ds. Kinnaird, and others, of note and notoriety. Like other parties of the kind, it was first silent, then talky, then argumentative, then disputatious, then unintelligible, then altogethery, then inarticulate, and then drunk. When we had reached the last step of this glorious ladder, it was difficult to get down again without stumbling; and to crown all, Kinnaird and I had to conduct Sheridan down a d—d corkscrew staircase, which had certainly been constructed before the discovery of fermented liquors, and to which no legs, however crooked, could possibly accommodate themselves. We deposited him safe at home, where his man, evidently used to the business, waited to receive him in the hall.

Both he and Colman were, as usual, very good; but I carried away much wine, and the wine had previously carried away my memory; so that all was hiccup and happiness for the last hour or so, and I am not impregnated with any of the conversation. Perhaps you heard of a late answer of Sheridan to the watchman who found him bereft of that 'divine particle of air', called reason ... He, the watchman, who found Sherry in the street, fuddled and bewildered, and almost insensible. 'Who are *you*, Sir?' – no answer. 'What's your name?' – a hiccup. 'What's your name?' – Answer, in a slow, deliberate and impassive tone – 'Wilberforce ! ! !' Is not that Sherry all over? – and, to my mind, excellent. Poor fellow, *his* very dregs are better than the 'first sprightly runnings' of others.

My paper is full, and I have a grievous headache.

Letter to Thomas Moore, 31 October 1815

He saluted Moore, later to become his biographer, in

*wine and that splendid quality of lyric that marks the
best of his poetry –*

> My boat is on the shore,
>   And my bark is on the sea;
> But, before I go, Tom Moore,
>   Here's a double health to thee!
>
> Here's a sigh to those who love me,
>   And a smile to those who hate
> And, whatever sky's above me,
>   Here's a heart for every fate.
>
> Though the ocean roar around me,
>   Yet it still shall bear me on;
> Though a desert shall surround me,
>   It hath springs that may be won.
>
> Were't the last drop in the well,
>   As I gasped upon the brink,
> Ere my fainting spirit fell,
>   'Tis to thee that I would drink.
>
> With that water, as this wine,
>   The libation I would pour
> Should be – peace with thine and mine,
>   And a health to thee, Tom Moore.
>
> 'To Thomas Moore', 1817

> The simple olives, best allies of wine,
>   Must I pass over in my bill of fare?
> I must, although a favourite 'plat' of mine
>   In Spain, and Lucca, Athens, everywhere:
> On them and bread 'twas oft my luck to dine,
>   The grass my table-cloth, in open air,
> On Sunium or Hymettus, like Diogenes,
> Of whom half my philosophy the progeny is.
>
> *Don Juan*, Canto XV

I think you told me, at Venice, that your spirits did
not keep up without a little claret. I *can* drink, and
bear a good deal of wine (as you may recollect in

England); but it don't exhilarate – it makes me savage and suspicious, and even quarrelsome. Laudanum has a similar effect; but I can take much of *it* without any effect at all. The thing that gives me the highest spirits (it seems absurd, but true) is a dose of *salts* – I mean in the afternoon, after their effect. But one can't take *them* like champagne.

Letter to Thomas Moore, 6 October 1821

We went down to Newstead together, where I had got a famous cellar, and Monks' dresses from a masquerade warehouse. We were a company of some seven or eight, with an occasional neighbour or so for visitors, and used to sit up late in our friars' dresses, drinking burgundy, claret, champagne, and what not, out of the skull-cup, and all sorts of glasses, and buffooning all round the house, in our conventional garments. Matthews always denominated me 'the Abbot', and never called me by any other name in his good humours, to the day of his death.

Letter to John Murray, 9 December 1820

Man, being reasonable, must get drunk;
    The best of life is but intoxication:
Glory, the grape, love, gold, in these are sunk
    The hopes of all men, and of every nation;
Without their sap, how branchless were the trunk
    Of life's strange tree, so fruitful on occasion!
But to return, – Get very drunk; and when
You wake with headache – you shall see what then.

Ring for your valet – bid him quickly bring
    Some hock and soda-water, then you'll know
A pleasure worthy Xerxes the great king;
    For not the blest sherbet, sublimed with snow,
Nor the first sparkle of the desert spring,
    Nor Burgundy in all its sunset glow,
After long travel, ennui, love, or slaughter,
Vie with that draught of hock and soda-water.

Don Juan, Canto II

Fill the goblet again! for I never before
Felt the glow which now gladdens my heart to
the core;
Let us drink! who would not? since, through life's
varied round,
In the goblet alone no deception is found.

In the days of my youth – when the heart's in its
spring
And dreams that affection can never take wing –
I had friends! who has not? but what tongue will
avow,
That friends, rosy wine! are so faithful as thou?

The heart of a mistress some boy may estrange,
Friendship shifts with the sunbeam, thou never
canst change;
Thou grow'st old, who does not? but on earth
what appears,
Whose virtues, like thine, still increase with its
years?

Yet, if blest to the utmost that love can bestow,
Should a rival bow down to our idol below,
We are jealous! who's not? thou hast no such alloy.
For the more that enjoy thee, the more we enjoy.

Then the season of youth and its vanities past,
For refuge we fly to the goblet at last;
There we find, do we not? in the flow of the soul,
That truth, as of yore, is confined to the bowl.

When the box of Pandora was opened on earth,
And Misery's triumph commenced over Mirth,
Hope was left, was she not? but the goblet we kiss,
And care not for Hope, who are certain of bliss.

Long life to the grape! for when summer is flown,
The age of our nectar shall gladden our own,
We must die! who shall not? May our sins be
      forgiven,
And Hebe shall never be idle in Heaven.

'Fill the Goblet Again', *c*. 1808

The Poetry of Wine

There is criticism not only of wine but of wine drinking, wine drinkers, and the effect of wine drinking.

Ultimately, though, it is justified on the highest level – that of the spirit (no pun intended, Brillat-Savarin notwithstanding). It has inspired poetry: poetry, that is, as distinct from verse or wit; and distinguished from both by that indefinable quality which goes to the heart. At least three passages – one from Rabelais' Gargantua, one by George Moore, and one by the American Nathaniel Hawthorne are in prose but their essence and their impact are those of poetry.

There has been much light versification on the subject; many a turn of a pretty phrase, but all these must fall before the truly poetic quality of the passages that follow. The majority of them are brief and it may be argued that there is no great sustained long poem on the subject. What cannot be gainsaid, however, is that in phrases, lines, even stanzas, poets have translated the often turbulent emotions of wine into the tranquillity of rich contemplation. These quotations call for little gloss; for their appeal is straight to the emotions. To discuss them technically or to subside to the level of heavy-handed linking is to do them, and the poets, a disservice – to come between them and the reader, like explaining the impact of a Krug champagne in terms of chemical analysis. The first, though, may be no more than a companionable threshold, the light touch of a time past.

> Souls of Poets dead and gone,
> What Elysium have ye known,
> Happy field or mossy cavern,
> Choicer than the Mermaid Tavern?

Have ye tippled drink more fine
Than mine host's Canary wine?
Or are fruits of Paradise
Sweeter than those dainty pies
Of venison? O generous food!
Drest as though bold Robin Hood
Would, with his maid Marian,
Sup and bowse from horn and can.

I have heard that on a day
Mine host's sign-board flew away,
Nobody knew whither, till
An astrologer's old quill
To a sheepskin gave the story,
Said he saw you in your glory,
Underneath a new old-sign
Sipping beverage divine,
And pledging with contented smack
The Mermaid in the Zodiac.

Souls of Poets dead and gone,
What Elysium have you known,
Happy field or mossy cavern,
Choicer than the Mermaid Tavern?

John Keats, 'Lines on the Mermaid Tavern', 1820

Ah, fill the Cup, what boots it to repeat
How time itself – slipping underneath our Feet:
Unborn To-morrow and dead Yesterday.
Why fret about them if To-day be sweet!

The Rubáiyát of Omar Khayyám, c. 1100,
trans. Edward Fitzgerald, 1895

The Spirit of Wine
Sang in my glass, and I listened
With love to his odorous music,
His flushed and magnificent song.

'I am health, I am heart, I am life!
For I give for the asking
The fire of my father the Sun,
And the strength of my mother the Earth.

Inspiration in essence,
I am wisdom and wit to the wise,
His visible muse to the poet,
The soul of desire to the lover,
The genius of laughter to all.'

W. E. Henley, 'The Spirit of Wine'

Then did they fall upon the chat of victuals, and some
belly furniture to be snatched at in the very same
place. Which purpose was no sooner mentioned, but
forthwith began flagons to go, gammons to trot,
goblets to fly, great bowls to ting, glasses to ring.
Draw, reach, fill, mix. So my friend, so, whip me off
this glass neatly, bring me hither some claret, a full
weeping glass till it run over. A cessation and truce with
thirst. Ha, thou false fever, wilt thou not be gone?
By my figgins, godmother, I cannot as yet enter in
the humour of being merry, nor drink so currently as
I would. By the belly of Sanct Buff, let us talk of our
drink: I never drink but at my hours, like the Pope's
mule. And I never drink but in my breviary, like a
fair father guardian. Which was first, thirst or drinking? Thirst, for who in the time of innocence would
have drunk without being athirst? Nay, sir, it was
drinking. We poor innocents drink but too much without thirst. Not I truly, who am a sinner, for I never
drink without thirst, either present or future. To
prevent it, as you know, I drink for the thirst to come.
I drink eternally. This is to me an eternity of drinking, and drinking of eternity. Let us sing, let us drink,
and tune up our roundlays. Where is my funnel? Do
you wet yourselves to dry, or do you dry to wet you?
Pish, I understand not the rhetoric (theoric I should
say), but I help myself somewhat by the practice.
Beast, enough! I sup, I wet, I humect, I moisten my
gullet, I drink and all for fear of dying. Drink always
and you shall never die. If I drink not, I am a ground
dry, gravelled and spent. I am stark dead without
drink, and my soul ready to fly into some marsh

amongst frogs: the soul never dwells in a dry place, drought kills it. O you butlers, creators of new forms, make me of no drinker a drinker, perenity and ever-lastingness of sprinkling, and bedewing me through these my parched and sinewy bowels. He drinks in vain, that feels not the pleasure of it. This entereth into my veins, the pissing tool and urinal vessels shall have nothing of it. I would willingly wash the tripes of the calf, which I appareled this morning. I have pretty well now ballasted my stomach, and stuffed my paunch. If the papers of my bonds and bills could drink as well as I do, my creditors would not want for wine when they come to see me. This hand of yours spoils your nose. O how many other such will enter here before this go out! What, drink so shallow? It is enough to break both girds and pettrel. This is called a cup of dissimulation, or flaggonal hypocrisy.

What difference is there between a bottle and a flagon? Great difference; for the bottle is stopped and shut up with a stopper, but the flagon with a vice. Bravely and well played upon the words! Our fathers drank lustily, and emptied their cans. Well cacked, well sung! Come, let us drink: will you send nothing to the river? Here is one going to wash the tripes. I drink no more than a sponge. I drink like a Templar Knight. Give me a synonymon for a gammon of bacon. It is the compulsory of drinkers: it is a pully. By a pully-rope wine is let down into the cellar and by a gammon into the stomach. Hey! now boys, hither, some drink, some drink.

François Rabelais, *Gargantua and Pantagruel*, 1534–64

The Wine is murmuring in the gloom,
Because he feels that Spring is come
To gladden everything outside . . .
To wing the dove to meet his bride
And not disdainfully to pass
Even the snail along the grass;

Because he feels that on the slope
Of his own hill the vine-flowers ope;
Because he feels that never more
Will earth or heaven *his* past restore.
He beats against the ribs of iron
Which him and all his strength environ;
He murmurs, swells, and beats again,
He murmurs, swells, and beats in vain ...

Walter Savage Landor, *c*. 1847

One eve in the bottle sang the soul of wine;
   'Man, unto thee, dear disinherited,
I sing a song of love and light divine –
   Prisoned in glass beneath my seals of red.

'I know thou labourest on the hill of fire,
   In sweat and pain beneath a flaming sun,
To give the life and soul my vines desire,
   And I am grateful for thy labours done.

'For I find joys unnumbered when I have
   The throat of man by travail long outworn,
And his hot bosom is a sweeter grave
   Of sounder sleep than my cold caves forlorn.

'Hearest thou not the echoing Sabbath sound?
   The hope that whispers in my trembling breast?
Thy elbows on the table! gaze around;
   Glorify me with joy and be at rest.

'To thy wife's eyes I'll bring their long-lost gleam,
   I'll bring back to thy child his strength and light,
To him, life's fragile athlete I will seem
   Rare oil that firms his muscles for the fight.

'I flow in man's heart as ambrosia flows;
   The grain the eternal Sower casts in the sod –
From our first loves the first fair verse arose,
   Flower-like aspiring to the heavens and God!'

Charles Baudelaire (1821–67), trans. F. P. Sturm

Wait not for the lamp; there is but a finger's breadth of day. Let us drink. Take the great cups from the rafters for Bacchus gave to man Wine that overcomes trouble. Let these be filled to overflowing with two measures of wine to one of water, and see there be no pause between each serving.

Alcateus, 600 BC

She gave him her hand and sat watching his lined face and his greying hair – a monk come out of the wilderness, she said; weary, hungry, and thirsty, no doubt. We have some wine; it will revive thee. And releasing her hand from his she fetched it; and hungry too, no doubt? I am too weary to eat, he answered, but will drink. As he sipped the wine she brought him, he told her of his arrival yesterday at Argenteuil, and how to his surprise and grief he found the convent closed. Why grief? she asked, and he answered her: Because I was eager to see thee. And then he related, in the broken words of a man overtired, who fetched his words with difficulty, that he had slept in the inn that night but gained little rest; for I was overtired and my sleep was short and starting. And despite thy tired limbs thou hast come to me? And have been seeking through Paris for thee, he interjected, at last to find thee; that is enough. But let me loosen thy cloak, she said let me relieve thee of it. And he let her do as she wished, and from his aching feet she drew the worn shoes.

George Moore, *Héloïse and Abélard*, 1921

'Tomaso, bring some Sunshine!' said [Donatello, Count of Monte Beni].

The readiest method of obeying this order, one might suppose, would have been to fling wide the green window blinds and let the glow of the summer noon into the carefully shaded room. But, at Monte Beni, with provident caution against the wintry days, when there is little sunshine, and the rainy ones, when there is none, it was the hereditary custom to keep their Sunshine stored away in the cellar. Old Tomaso quickly produced some of it in a small, straw-covered flask.

'This is a wine,' observed the Count, 'the secret of making which has been kept in our family for centuries upon centuries; nor would it avail any man to steal the secret, unless he could also steal the vineyard, in which alone the Monte Beni grape can be produced. There is little else left me, save that patch of vines. Taste some of their juice, and tell me whether it is worthy to be called Sunshine, for that is its name.'

'A glorious name, too!' cried [Kenyon].

'Taste it,' said Donatello, filling his friend's glass, and pouring likewise a little into his own. 'But first smell its fragrance; for the wine is very lavish of it, and will scatter it all abroad.'

'Ah, how exquisite!' said Kenyon. 'No other wine has a bouquet like this. The flavour must be rare, indeed, if it fulfill the promise of this fragrance...'

This invaluable liquor was of a pale golden hue, like other of the rarest Italian wines, and, if carelessly and irreligiously quaffed, might have been mistaken for a very fine sort of champagne. It was not, however, an effervescing wine, although its delicate piquancy produced a somewhat similar effect upon the palate. Sipping, the guest longed to sip again; but the wine demanded so deliberate a pause, in order to detect the hidden peculiarities and subtle exquisiteness of its flavour, that to drink it was really more a moral than a physical enjoyment...

'This is surely the wine of the Golden Age, such as Bacchus himself first taught mankind to press from the choicest of his grapes. My dear Count, why is it not illustrious? The pale, liquid gold in every such flask as that might be solidified into golden scudi, and would quickly make you a millionaire!'

Tomaso, the old butler, who was standing by the

table, and enjoying the praises of the wine quite as much as if bestowed upon himself, made answer:

'We have a tradition, signore,' said he, 'that this rare wine of our vineyard would lose all its wonderful qualities, if any of it were sent to market. The Counts of Monte Beni have never parted with a single flask of it for gold. At their banquets, in the olden time, they have entertained princes, cardinals, and once an emperor, and once a pope, with this delicious wine, and always, even to this day, it has been their custom to let it flow freely, when those whom they love and honour sit at the board. But the grand duke himself could not drink that wine, except it were under this very roof!'...

'To speak out all the truth, there is an excellent reason why neither a cask nor a flask of our precious vintage should ever be sent to market. The wine, signore, is so fond of its native home that a transportation of even a few miles turns it quite sour. And yet it is a wine that keeps well in the cellar underneath this floor, and gathers fragrance, flavour, and brightness in its dark dungeon. That very flask of Sunshine, now, has kept itself for you, sir, guest (as a maid reserves her sweetness till her lover comes for it), ever since a merry vintage time when the Signore Count here was a boy!'

'You must not wait for Tomaso to end his discourse about the wine, before drinking off your glass,' observed Donatello. 'When once the flask is uncorked, its finest qualities lose little time in making their escape. I doubt whether your last sip will be quite so delicious as you found the first.'

And, in truth, the sculptor fancied that the Sunshine became almost imperceptibly clouded, as he approached the bottom of the flask. The effect of the wine, however, was a gentle exhilaration, which did not so speedily pass away.

Nathaniel Hawthorne, *The Marble Faun*, 1860

A little saint best fits a little shrine,
A little prop best fits a little vine,
As my small cruse best fits my little wine.

> Robert Herrick, 'Upon a Pipkin of Jelly sent to a
> Lady', *Hesperides*, 1648

'But enough of war and its victories. Apollo, now shedding his armour, bids me attune my lyre to songs of peace. Let the leafy grove be filled with feasters clad in the white robes befitting the festive occasion. Place a garland of roses about my head. Let wine crushed in Falernian presses flow freely. Let the poet, inspired by wine, call upon his muse for songs of joy and laughter. Bacchus 'tis thy pleasure to hold the hours of darkness for the coming of Apollo. Thus will I pass the night with drink and good cheer 'till dawn shall cast golden bars across the purple of my wine.'

> Propertius, *c.* 20 BC

... thy mouth like the best wine for my beloved, that goeth down sweetly, causing the lips of those that are asleep to speak.

> The Song of Solomon 7: 9

I within did flow
With seas of life, like wine.

> Thomas Traherne (1638–74), 'Wonder', *Poems*, 1908

And David's Lips are lock't but in Divine,
High-piping Pehlevi, with Wine ! Wine! Wine!
   'Red Wine' – the Nightingale cries to the Rose
That yellow cheek of hers t'incardine.

> *The Rubáiyát of Omar Khayyám, c,* 1100
> trans. Edward Fitzgerald, 1859

Behold the Lord maketh the earth empty ... the inhabitants of the earth are burned, and few men left.

The new wine mourneth, the vine languisheth, all the merry-hearted do sigh.

The mirth of tabrets ceaseth, the noise of them that rejoiceth endeth, the joy of the harp ceaseth.

They shall not drink wine with a song; strong drink shall be bitter to them that drink it.

The city of confusion is broken down: every house is shut up that no man may come in.

There is a crying for wine in the streets; all joy is darkened, and the mirth of the land is gone.

Isaiah 24: 6–11

What though youth gave love and roses,
Age still leaves us friends and wine.

Thomas Moore (1779–1852)

And if the Wine you drink, the Lip you press,
End in the Nothing all things end in – Yes –
  Then fancy while thou art, Thou art but what
Thou shalt be – Nothing – though shalt not be less.

The Rubáiyát of Omar Khayyám, c. 1100,
trans. Edward Fitzgerald, 1859

It is my wish to die in an inn; let wine be placed to the lips of the dying man, so that, when they come, the choruses of angels may say 'God be kind to this drinker'.

Canon Walter Map (or Mapes),
De Nugis Curialium, c. 1200

Acknowledgements

The editor and publishers gratefully acknowledge permission to use copyright material in this book:

Martin Armstrong: 'Hock', and 'Burgundy', from *Wine and Food Society Journal*, No. 5, 1935.

Eric Chilman: 'Claret is King' from *Wine and Food Society Journal*.

Colette: from 'Prisons et Paradis', trans. Derek Coltman, from *Earthly Paradise* ed. Robert Phelps. Copyright © 1966 by Farrar, Straus & Giroux, Inc. Reprinted by permission of Martin Secker & Warburg Ltd., and Farrar, Straus & Giroux, Inc.

Patrick Forbes: from *Champagne* (1967). Reprinted by permission of Victor Gollancz Ltd.

Hugh Johnson: from *Wine* (Mitchell Beazley, Ltd., 1966).

Christopher Marsden: from *Palmyra of the North: The First Days of St. Petersburg* (Faber, 1942). Reprinted by permission of the author.

Edmund Penning-Rowsell: from *The Wines of Bordeaux* (Allen Lane/Penguin, 1979). Reprinted by permission of the author.

Raymond Postgate: from *The Plain Man's Guide to Wine* (1951). Reprinted by permission of Michael Joseph.

Cyril Ray: from *In A Glass Lightly* (1967). Reprinted by permission of the author.

J. M. Scott: from *The Vineyards of France* (Hodder, 1950). Reprinted by permission of A. P. Watt Ltd., on behalf of J. M. Scott, OBE.

André Simon: from the Introduction to *How to Enjoy Wine* (Newman Neame, 1952) and from the *Introduction to a Wine Primer* (Michael Joseph, 1946).

While every effort has been made to secure permission, we may have failed in a few cases to trace the copyright holder. We apologize for any apparent negligence.

ACKNOWLEDGEMENTS

The illustrations in this book were taken from the following sources: Jean-Anthelme Brillat-Savarine, *La Physiologie du Goût* (1825); C. Cocks and E. Feret, *Bordeaux et ses Vins* (Bordeaux, 1949); C. S. Gutkind and K. Wolfskehl, *Das Buch vom Wein* (Munich, 1927); Clarence P. Hornung, *Handbook of Early Advertising Art* (New York, 1956); R. S. Surtees, *Handley Cross* (London, 1854); Irving Zucker, *A Source Book of French Advertising Art* (London, 1970).

Index

Adams, Franklin, 27
Alcateus, 104
Aldrich, Henry, 9
Anacreon, 5–6, 8
Anonymous, 22–3, 31, 49, 90, 91–2
Apperley, C. J., 85–6
Armstrong, Martin, 56–7, 64–5
Athenaeus, 11, 31, 92

Baudelaire, Charles, 103
Beaumont, Francis, 30
Bernard, John, 84–5
Bible, viii, 4–5, 8, 12, 21, 22, 27, 74, 107–8
Bierce, Ambrose, 30, 73
Blackie, John Stuart, 90
Boorde, Andrew, 33–4
Boswell, James, 28–30, 74–5
Breton, Nicholas, 73
Brillat-Savarin, Jean-Anthelme, 17–19
Burns, Robert, 88–9
Butler, Samuel, 23
Byron, George Gordon Noel, Lord, 33, 50, 93–8

Cervantes, Miguel de, 91
Chaucer, Geoffrey, 21
Chesterfield, Earl of, 42
Chilman, Eric, 51
Cockburn, Henry, Lord, 81–2
Coggan, Thomas, 30
Coleridge, Samuel Taylor, 90
Colette, 34–5
Cowley, Abraham, 8
Crabbe, George, 12

Daudet, Alphonse, 60–1
Dickens, Charles, 81

Euripides 92

Fitzgerald, Edward, *see* Khayyám. Omar
Fletcher, John, 12–13, 30
Forbes, Patrick, 46–9
Fuller, Thomas, 23

Gay, John, 21, 52–3
George, IV, 77
Gronow, Capt. R. H., 40

Hawthorne, Nathaniel, 104–6
Henley, W. E., 100–1
Herbert, George, 32, 74
Herrick, Robert, 107
Homer, 12

Jerrold, Douglas, 91
Johnson, Hugh, 53–4, 58–60, 61–2, 66–7
Johnson, Samuel, 28–30, 74–5
Jonson, Ben, 8–9

Keats, John, 6, 12, 51–2, 99–100
Khayyám, Omar, 7, 10–11, 15, 100, 107, 108

Landor, Walter Savage, 102–3
Leybourne, George, 42–3
Li T'ai Po, 7, 31
Lithgow, William, 11
Longfellow, Henry Wadsworth, 70–2
Luttrell, Henry, 50

Map, Canon Walter, 108
Marsden, Christopher, 87
Meredith, George, 68–9
Michelet, Jules, 43
Milton, John, 24–5
Minsheu, John, 11
Moore, George, 104
Moore, Thomas, 50, 108

Nimrod, *see* Apperley, C. J.

O'Keeffe, John, 82–3
Ovid, 30–1

Panyasis, 26
Peacock, Thomas Love, 10,
 90, 91
Penning-Rowsell, Edmund,
 54–6
Peter the Great, 86–7
Phillips, Stephen, 13
Pitt, William, the Younger,
 77–8
Postgate, Raymond, 15–17
Praed, Winthrop Mackworth,
 19–20
Propertius, 107
Purcell, Henry, 92

Rabelais, François, 11, 101–2
Ralegh, Sir Walter, 25–6
Ray, Cyril, 57–8, 62–3, 65–6
Rochester, Earl, of, 19

Rogers, Samuel, 77–8, 83

Sainsbury, George, 13–14,
 40–1
Scott, J. M., 36–8
Shakespeare, William, 21, 32,
 39–40
Shaw, T. G., 75–7
Simon, André, 1–4
Steele, Sir Richard, 78–80
Surtees, R. S., 69–70

Tennyson, Alfred Lord, 15
Thackeray, William
 Makepeace, 44–5
Thoreau. Henry, 38
Traherne, Thomas, 107
Treves, Bishop of, 88

Virgil, 6
Voltaire, 44

Walpole, Sir Robert, 77
Webster, John, 13
Wilde, Oscar, 90